CELEBRATE
the JOURNEY

Discovering God's Vision for Your Life

DEBRA FULGHUM BRUCE & ELLEN OLDACRE

CPH.
SAINT LOUIS

Copyright © 2000 Concordia Publishing House
3558 S. Jefferson Avenue
St. Louis, MO 63118-3968
Manufactured in the United States of America

Library of Congress Cataloging-in-Publication Data
Bruce, Debra Fulghum, 1951–
Celebrate the journey : discovering God's vision for your life / Debra Fulghum Bruce
and Ellen Oldacre.
p. cm.
ISBN 0-570-05244-0
1. Christian women—Religious life. I. Oldacre, Ellen W. II. Title.
BV4527.B78 2000
248.8′43—dc21   99-059018

1 2 3 4 5 6 7 8 9 10   09 08 07 06 05 04 03 02 01 00

This is dedicated to the
special women in our lives:

Our mothers—Jewel Holden Fulghum and
Myrtle Jordan Welch

Our sisters—Linda McIlwain and
Lori Steinmeyer

Our daughters—Brittnye, Ashley, and
Claire Bruce; and Emily Lamkin

Our precious friends and mentors—Candy
Solomon and Debbie Harned

May they celebrate every day
of their special journeys.

Contents

Prologue

*M*any women openly agree that their lives and dreams for the future are so intertwined with reaching a specific goal or destination that any derived pleasure is disregarded. The destination may be trying to get your toddler toilet trained, or helping your teenager raise his math grade. The goal could be a job promotion, a vacation home, or early retirement. Commonly, our destinations are focused on our children becoming independent, or becoming debt-free with our spouse. However, the problems arise when *arriving* becomes the sole purpose of living and overshadows God's daily plan for our lives.

As we await this elusive destination, the calendar serves as an unerring measurement of time. Not surprisingly, while we run the harried, unsettled pace of life, most of us fail to pause and cherish the young child playing with her new puppy. The toddler's unending "why" questions are ignored as we busily push through the day. Even the intimate talks with our teenager, spouse, or best friend are not fully appreciated as we constantly have our mind on the next item on our daily "to do" list. Sadly, our own personal dreams and talents are often put on "hold" as we hurriedly get through the day to meet our long-term goal. And the changing seasons are but a faint memory as our lives transport us swiftly across the years. Instead of cherishing the moment and God's provision for our lives, we become hypnotically affixed to the destination—that captivating point that always remains just beyond our ever-weakening grasp.

How about you? Have you said the following?

- If only we had more money, we'd be so happy.
- If only we could buy that larger house, our troubles would be over.
- When I get my promotion, this job will be so much better.
- I can't wait for the day when she is able to dress herself.
- When we pay off the college loans, I will feel relaxed.
- I will sing in the choir when my kids get older.
- I studied art in college but there's no way I can paint now with the kids at home.

And the list goes on.

While having a destination or goal in life is important, we also can learn to savor the moment by discovering and celebrating God's vision for our lives. Each of us is His precious child, bought by the saving blood of Jesus Christ, and He has a plan for us. " 'For I know the plans I have for you,' declares the LORD, 'plans to prosper you and not to harm you, plans to give you hope and a future' " (Jeremiah 29:11). We trust in His plan for us, we cherish each day's journey, even in times of despair. "And we know that in all things God works for the good of those who love Him, who have been called according to His purpose. ... We are more than conquerors through Him who loves us" (Romans 8:28, 37). That's good news for all of us! This book is about *vision*. As you move through your life, where is your focus? We are reminded in Hebrews, "Let us fix our eyes on Jesus, the author and perfecter of our faith, who for the joy set before Him endured the cross, scorning its shame, and sat down at the right hand of the throne of God. Consider Him who endured so much opposition from sinful men, so that you will not grow weary and lose heart" (12:2–3). In the coming pages we will talk about being "women of vision." We are women of vision when we "fix our eyes on Jesus," the Savior who walked the way of the cross and has called us to follow where He leads.

It is our prayer that this book will help you "renew your prescription" and keep your eyes on your Savior as the "author and perfecter of our faith."

Deb and Ellen

PART ONE:
Celebrations and Concerns

CHAPTER 1

Beyond Stereotypes

It's no news to you by now that the only thing certain in life is change. Think about it. Through the passing of time, our children change as they move from dependence to independence. Our parents change as they age and become more dependent. Even we change—our hair thins and changes colors; our bodies change shape; and our height changes as the effects of aging take hold.

Sometimes change is exciting—the birth of a child or grandchild, moving into a new home, or starting a new career. Yet so often change is not a welcomed event. In our fast-paced society, framed by the chaos of millennium madness, we begin to fear change. Journalists, statisticians, futurists, and preachers point their fingers at the doom and gloom changes marring our nation. Still, in God's design for the world and for our lives, change is a constant. While it's only human to want to hold onto things just as they are in order to feel comfortable and safe, God knows that in order to mature and grow, we must get out of our comfort zones and lean on Him. As Harry Emerson Fosdick once said, "Christians are supposed not merely to endure change, nor even to profit by it, but to cause it." Yes, we are called to make a difference because God has made such a difference in our own lives!

Before we talk about celebrating the journey of your life, let's first consider how many things change to become more useful or beautiful.

- The caterpillar changes into a butterfly.
- A tadpole becomes a frog.
- A tree becomes the paper we use every day.
- Grapes become raisins.
- Tomatoes become pizza sauce.
- Little girls become women.
- Women become leaders, encouragers, prayer warriors, sisters, mothers, and wives.

God is constantly working in us—transforming us, if you will. In fact, He has already transformed us into new creatures through Baptism.

You are probably familiar with Psalm 139:13–14, "For You created my inmost being; You knit me together in my mother's womb. I praise You because I am fearfully and wonderfully made; Your works are wonderful, I know that full well." As parents, we teach this concept to our children. But do we really believe it about ourselves?

There is not one precious baby who was more fearfully and wonderfully made than you were. You are a child of God. He loves you and has chosen you for His own. As a child of God, you have amazing potential and possibility—

no matter where you are in life. You likely give of yourself to your family, career, friends, church, and community. You join the ranks of a multitude of women through the ages who have given of their very beings to care for children, to manage homes, to stand beside husbands, or to sacrificially serve Christ through their church, community, and country. Consider the following.

You join hands with Jachobed, the mother of Moses, whose God-given ingenuity and obedience saved her son from death. She thought out her plan and had the courage to follow through. She will forever be remembered as the mother of Aaron, Moses, and Miriam.

You stand in the same line with women like Susannah Wesley who weathered financial difficulties, illness, public harassment, and the loss of nine children to profoundly affect the spiritual awakening in England in the early 1700s. To provide the best positive Christian witness for her family and to know and understand her children, Susannah vowed to spend an hour a week one on one with each of her nine living offspring. Her powerful influence on her children gave us John and Charles Wesley whose leadership helped to bring the Gospel to America.

You walk side by side with women like Fran, who grew up attending a one-room schoolhouse in a small Midwestern town, but after several years of seeking God's direction, moved to a large urban area to receive more education. She pursued a master's degree and a doctorate and now works as an academic counselor in the athletic department of a university. She is challenging young people to make a difference in their lives and in the world. As many of these college students come to her with complicated, searching questions, she shares her faith and her own struggles and walk with the Lord. She creates programs and classes to strengthen her students academically and socially, no matter what their background. She loves them as they try to overcome backgrounds and use their God-given gifts. On Sundays you will find her active in her church, sharing her gift of music with a ministry to the homeless or playing the piano for her Sunday school class. Through Fran, the light of Christ shines brightly.

You put your arm around Joan, single mother of three girls. When Joan couldn't make enough money to make ends meet, she prayed for a way to meet her young family's financial demands. She began making crafts to sell in local craft shows in her town and nearby counties. As her daughters grew, Joan encouraged them to help with the "business." After several years of working all day, taking care of her girls, and working on crafts at night, Joan's efforts paid off. Today she owns and operates her own craft store and mail-order business. Her daughters work with her after school and at craft fairs. Joan's girls have a strong work ethic. They understand what God can do to change lives.

We thank God for the faithful witness of these women—the strength and gladness with which they performed their tasks.

Welcome to the "Women's Hall of Fame"

Because you are *you*, you're already a member of the "Women's Hall of Fame." We voted you in for every shoe you have tied, for every meeting you have organized, for every hand you have held, for every back you have patted, and for every supportive prayer you have prayed. Throughout history, God has used ordinary women, like all of us, to do extraordinary things for Him. Their stories are woven into this book. But this book is about *you*. It is about who you are and who you want to become. It is about seeing beyond the dirty dishes, the diapers, the briefcases, and the make-up to find a woman who knows how to hope, believe, and dream. We aren't talking about the sweet, romantic, happily-ever-after dreams. We are talking about enjoying life as a child of God, who gave us the gift of all creation and the Gift of Himself, who enters our lives and stays front and center. In Him we are freed from the guilt which so often holds us back. Women of vision understand the difference between wishing and living the life of peace and joy with which God blesses us.

It's Not Your Mother's Vision

Where there is no vision, the people perish.
Proverbs 29:18 KJV

The verse in Psalms says you are fearfully and wonderfully made. It doesn't say you are made to be your mother, or your mother-in-law, or your grandmother, or your sister, or your neighbor, or the girls in your Bible study group. It says *you*. One of our biggest obstacles to clear vision is the comparison game. How many of these statements sound familiar?

• If only I had her home, I know I'd be happier.

• If only I were thinner, my clothes would look better.

- If only I had completed college, I would be considered for a promotion.
- If only I had married someone else, I would know what true love really is.
- If only my hips were smaller (or legs or arms or waist!), I'd be truly satisfied with my body.
- If only I had been born into a different family, I would have had more opportunities in life.

And the list goes on.

Isn't it amazing how we criticize what God made? He knits us together in our mothers' wombs and knows the exact number of hairs on our heads. Still, we tell Him we are not good enough. He made you unique. You are one of a kind. God didn't intend for you to be like anyone else. He is not waiting until you look like Barbie to give you clearer "vision" for your life. It doesn't matter to Him if you are married or single; He has a plan for you and He will provide all you need. God does not check to see if you are a CEO or a mom who homeschools. His desire is for you to become all He created you to be.

Be Thou My Vision

Ellen remembers a "vision experience" that happened to her as a teenager.

I had just started wearing contacts. They were the old, hard kind of lenses. For some reason, I was standing in front of the mirror in my parents' bedroom. As I tried to put one in, it fell off my finger and down toward the carpet. Those were the

days of shag carpet. You can imagine how diffi-
cult it was to search for one little blue contact in
shag carpet. We searched and searched in vain.
There was no way I could see and function with
just one contact. I was in tears, and as I often did
when I needed comforting, I bent down to hug
my dog. There, on good old Susie Q's back of
brown and white short fur, was my contact. She
had passed by the dresser just at the exact second
the contact fell. What were the odds of that hap-
pening? There was no way I could see clearly.
Literally, my vision was taken away!

Think of times when your vision was blurred, either literally or figuratively. What happened? When we start comparing ourselves with others instead of asking God to help us discover who He wants us to be, we have no chance of seeing clearly. We create unrealistic standards for ourselves. It is possible to learn about yourself, and set new goals for your life without guilt—Christ has freed us from that guilt through His death and resurrection.

And still, we beat ourselves up. With which of the following problems do you most identify?

Problem: You love to buy and read women's magazines, but every time you do, you feel horrible about
your body and yourself.

Solutions:

1. Don't buy them anymore (the obvious solution).
2. Determine you want to live a healthy lifestyle. Change
   your eating and exercise habits to protect yourself
   from disease and live longer. Remember, the cover girl

for *Glamour* may be skinny, but she may not be healthy.

Problem: You read a book about a successful business-woman who carries a nice leather, initialed briefcase and moves up the career ladder to become a CEO. You feel like a failure because although you work hard at your job, you know you will never get to live out your dream and be the head of the company.

Solutions:

1. Go out and buy yourself a nice briefcase and stuff it with whatever you would like!

2. Decide if you enjoy your level of professional involve-ment. If you don't, set goals to make a career move. If you do, find smarter ways to be productive and look for ways to reach out to your coworkers. Making a last-ing difference in the lives of those you work with can give new direction and motivation to an otherwise stale situation. Maybe you are not there to move up the ladder. Maybe you are there to help God move in your coworkers' lives.

Problem: You go to the Sunday school class party at Lorin's house and sit there the whole time feeling sorry for yourself. Even though you and your hus-band work hard, you can't afford anything Lorin has. Her children go to private school. She heads the Girl Scout citywide fund-raiser each year. Before you leave, you are feeling overwhelmingly guilty that your girls will never have the opportunities Lorin's children are afforded. You never want to have the class over to your house after they have been to Lorin's.

Solutions:

1. Don't go back to Lorin's until you can enjoy the fellowship instead of enduring the wealth.
2. Walk around your home and write down the things that are special to you. Include family members, pictures, books, gifts, and anything that has meaning to you.
3. Think about the people who have significantly impacted your life and your family's lives. Look at the list of things you wrote down. Thank God that He has blessed you with timeless, priceless things and people.

Problem: A nationally known Christian parenting expert leads a seminar at your church. After attending, you feel like you have failed your children and will never be a good mother. You are afraid of how your children will turn out.

Solutions:

1. Realize that a parenting expert knows a great deal about the parent and child relationship and can offer helpful advice, but he or she does not know your children. God has called you to be the expert at raising your children.
2. Take an honest look at your lifestyle and your children's behavior. Are you too busy? Or are you so focused on your own family that your children need more experience helping others?
3. Accept that there are no perfect parents, no perfect children, and no perfect families. Because of our sinful nature, we can't be perfect. But we have hope in

the One who is perfect—Jesus Christ. Pray to your heavenly Father, asking Him to help you be the best parent you can be.

4. If you see that you need to make changes, talk to your husband about them. Together, commit to make them because you believe it will help your family, not because you are conforming to everything a speaker said. Adapt advice to your family's personality and schedule.

5. Pray for your children every day. Pray specifically about different areas of their lives. For example, On Monday, pray for their teachers. On Tuesday, pray for their interactions with friends. On Wednesday, pray for their character. On Thursday, pray that they would come to have a deep relationship with Jesus Christ that would grow throughout their lives. On Friday, pray for your relationship with them. On Saturday, pray for their future decisions. On Sunday, pray for those leaders at your church who invest their time and love to help your children understand God's love for them.

The Danger of Worldwide Wrestling

The bell has rung. The opponents come out of their corners. One looks like you. And as we get a better view, the other one looks like you too! One of the biggest dangers of playing the comparison game is that you never let yourself win—and it's a constant battle. Your biggest foe continues to be you. How long can you survive beating yourself up for past mistakes, for not being like someone else, or for the differences which make you an individual? What good does it do to keep punishing yourself? What happens to a person when she keeps fighting with herself?

- Dragging yourself down seldom motivates you to push beyond yourself and find out what else you are capable of doing.
- It causes you to feel guilty.
- Unrealistic guilt causes bitterness and anger.
- To feel some relief from your guilt, you try to put others down.
- You become stagnant and immobile.
- You turn into your own worst enemy.

We are all sinful—we all have things to overcome. And we are able to overcome them because Christ overcame sin and death for us. It is in the overcoming that we learn tenacity, strength, and compassion for others. It is in the overcoming that our vision improves and we are able to see new opportunities.

Pleased or Pleaser?

Anne Graham Lotz has shared that growing up in Billy Graham's home brought challenges for her, especially during adolescence. Anne recalls, "I felt pressure to please everyone. People wanted me to measure up to what they thought I should be, and their standards were not necessarily always biblical or right. I almost cracked under the pressure. As a teenager, I attended a retreat and realized that I was looking at God through a prism relationship, colored by what others thought of me. I made the decision to live out my faith for God and to please Him and the people

I cared about the most. That has set the tone for my whole life. What I care about is what God thinks, not what other people think."

We know what God thinks. He made you. He gifted you. He sent His only Son to die for you. He wants to give you purpose and clear vision.

Today, Anne Graham Lotz is a tremendous Bible teacher and speaker. Her vision and ministry are changing lives all over the world. As Anne shared, "I learned about a steadfast commitment to faithfulness and integrity from my dad, and I learned to treasure the Bible from my mother. Just from the way she holds it, reads it, and obeys it, I know Mother has a real and precious love for the Lord. The demonstration of that love is at the core of my wanting a growing relationship with Him. It is the reason I have been doing what I do for 23 years now through a Bible-teaching ministry."

Ruth Bell Graham has been a constant overcomer throughout her life. Over the years of raising children alone, world travel, supporting Billy and the crusade ministry, enduring illness, and surviving many other obstacles, Ruth remains an inspiration. One cannot remember and affirm Billy Graham without thinking of the woman who has encouraged him and stood beside him in his ministry. You may stand beside a spouse, children, aging parents, coworkers, and friends every day, offering love, care, and support. You battle your own physical problems and deal with memories you must constantly overcome. Ask God to help you see your difficulties as opportunities.

Now for the Metamorphosis

Be careful. Don't read about the women of vision in this book and determine you can never be like them. They were, and are, ordinary women like you and like us. Few of them have ever been wealthy; few of them have ever been without difficulties. At some point in their lives, all women of vision have called out in desperation to God, asking Him to show them something more. God is in the change business. He is the creator of metamorphosis. Only a creative God could design the metamorphic change between a caterpillar and a butterfly. Let's look at the caterpillar and see if we can gain insights into who we are and who we want to become.

Caterpillars can be quite ugly. Have you ever seen a close-up of their bodies and mouths? They possess strong, biting jaws that differ from the sucking mouth of a butterfly. These little guys are heavy eaters. It is during the caterpillar stage that a butterfly or moth does all its growing, storing up the nutrients that later are used to transform it into an adult insect. If you are like us, you probably feel like you spend much more time being a caterpillar than an adult insect. Nevertheless, in God's plan for you and the caterpillar, this can be the most productive time. It is during our "not so lovely" stages that God teaches us some of the most valuable truths about ourselves, others, and His love. Even when we act like the segmented, creepy, crawling caterpillar, God wants to show us insights and use us to make a difference. He is preparing us for the day we grow wings and are ready to fly. If we never crawl around slowly as caterpillars, we will not appreciate the burst of color and freedom as we learn to take flight.

An art activity our children enjoyed when they were younger was making butterflies from a pattern of their feet. Try it. Put two bare feet side by side on a piece of paper. Trace the outline of the feet and toes. The feet pattern forms a butterfly that can be painted or colored. Antennae and a head can be added for additional effect. When the feet are traced on the paper, they are just ordinary feet. When color and shape are added, they are transformed into a wonderful butterfly. It takes some work and time to make the butterfly appear out of the footprint. That's what God does for each of us. He will do more with your life and your gifts than you ever dreamed possible.

Now to Him who is able to do immeasurably more than all we ask or imagine, according to His power that is at work within us, to Him be glory in the church and in Christ Jesus throughout all generations, for ever and ever! Amen. Ephesians 3:20–21

Caterpillars have built-in defense mechanisms. It is difficult for hatched caterpillars to ever mature to adult stage. Larger animals eat them and tiny parasitic wasp and fly larvae feed within their bodies and eventually kill caterpillars. Still, in His grand design scheme, God did not create the caterpillar totally helpless. Some caterpillars secrete an unpleasant fluid, others simply taste bad enough that birds and other animals find them sickening. A few kinds are covered with sharp spines filled with stinging fluids that can be injected into a person's skin. Others have false eyespots to assist in frightening away an attacker, and some have long, whip-like appendages on their backs to use in defense.

We doubt you were given any of these defense mechanisms. You were created with a higher ability to defend yourself from what might harm you. God created you with a mind to reason, to plan, to evaluate. God gave you a conscience. The Holy Spirit uses your conscience to help you know what is right and wrong. God's rules are not just some arbitrary *don'ts* created to make us "walk the line." They were created to protect us from emotional, mental, physical, and spiritual harm and to keep our vision clear.

We have a huge variety of available support to strengthen us in our defense against becoming visionless.

Read books that affirm your strengths and strengthen you in areas where you are weak. Read books and magazines that help you evaluate where you are and where you want to be. Read books that celebrate you as a creation of God. Find tangible support through a local church—a church that believes in family and the family of God reaching out to help one another; a church that challenges you to get out of your comfort zone and sharpen your vision for ministry. Become an active part of that church's ministry. Surround yourself with people who cause you to want to be all you can become. Guard against sharing pessimism. Become active and excited about your vision—you won't have time for gossip or making judgment calls about the lives of others. Find a prayer partner who is honest about where she is and where she is going.

Caterpillars are part of an ongoing life cycle. A butterfly produces tiny eggs that hatch into hungry caterpillars. Although the caterpillar spends most of its time eating and growing, its skin does not grow. The caterpillar sheds its skin and grows a larger one several times. After the caterpillar grows to its full size, it forms a protective shell or cocoon. While inside the shell, an incredible change occurs. The slow, creeping, worm-like caterpillar metamorphoses into a beautiful butterfly. The shell breaks open to unleash the butterfly to fly away and find a mate and produce another generation of butterfly eggs.

Join the Spiritual Life Cycle

You are not just one woman with singular vision. In the magnitude of God's plan, you are part of a magnificent spiritual life cycle. Little girls grow to become women of vision and share that vision in such a way that they impact the next generation. With God's help we change from scraped-kneed little girls to searching teenagers, to young adults with hopes and dreams, to adult women of wisdom, experience, maturity, and vision.

Do you know that there are approximately 15,000 to 20,000 species of butterflies? Likewise, no two women go through the life cycle the same way or with the same vision. We are all different. God gives each of us opportunities and allows each of us to make mistakes. Yet a woman of vision keeps going, keeps moving. She demonstrates her dependence on God to her children and those who surround her. She is not only a survivor, she learns to thrive. She wants something more.

Aha! God Likes Surprises

Dana cried for three days after her last child married and moved away. The house was so empty. She was left with no one to talk to and, even worse, no one to need her. For years she centered her life around her family. She never missed a football game or a choral concert. She made sure the family ate together as much as possible. She chaperoned school events and never missed church youth camp. Now, the most she could do was send care packages to her children or call them. Nothing was the same. She felt useless. In her desperation, Dana cried out to God to help her and to use her. God surprised her with a fun and unique opportunity to meet the needs of hundreds of people.

Dana was a first-class gardener. She designed her farm acreage with miles of English country gardens and a huge vegetable garden. Each year, Dana canned vegetables and gave them to family and friends for Christmas. Dana employed a man to help her tend all the gardens. One week, he called her to say he could not come out to the farm because he was putting his father in a nursing home. She knew the family had very little extra money. After the man returned to work, she inquired about the nursing home arrangements and discovered it was a special facility for low-income patients. Her garden helper expressed grave concern that his father would be well cared for and find any kind of joy in the rundown, dreary facility.

One afternoon, Dana picked a bouquet of flowers for the man to take to his father. The next week, she sent fresh vegetables and a jar of her special strawberry jam. The man reported that his father was the star of the nursing home.

The bouquet ended up on the table in the dining hall to brighten the otherwise bland surroundings. The strawberry jam was shared among the patients each morning at breakfast and the dining hall cooks fixed a special dish with the vegetables. As Dana began to send more bundles from her garden, she involved others from her church. She organized a group of gardeners who rotated bringing flowers, hanging baskets, food, and specialty baked goods for the patients to enjoy. Dana went every Saturday and put fresh flowers on each table in the dining hall to make Sunday dinner more special. Ministering to the patients at the home became her part-time volunteer job.

Dana wanted clearer vision. God surprised her by using what she already enjoyed to brighten the lives of others. The local newspaper praised her as a "woman of vision." Her reward comes from the faces of the patients and the staff at the nursing home.

"For I know the plans I have for you," declares the LORD, "plans to prosper you and not to harm you, plans to give you hope and a future." Jeremiah 29:11

Get with the Plan

When we were growing up, many preachers and youth speakers taught that God had a blueprint for our lives and our job was to discover His will for us. We grew to believe that God's will was the one major plan we had to find and then we could begin to live it. Wrong! While we believe that God has a plan for each of us, we also believe that His will begins now and happens every day of our lives. God's plan for you includes the way you sing "Jesus Loves Me" to your baby every time you rock her. God's plan for you includes the way you listened to your neighbor after her mother died. God's plan for you may involve your garden or your home or your office. God's plan is now. Even when we make mistakes, God doesn't toss out His plan and He certainly doesn't toss us out. We are His through Baptism and we are renewed in His grace every day. There are times our decisions cause us to miss the biggest blessings He has in store for us, but He creates new blessings and forgives us through Christ's death and resurrection.

Charting a New Course

"The real voyage of discovery consists not in seeking new landscapes but in having new eyes." Proust

Your world may be in transition or it may seem overwhelmingly lonely and mundane. You may face mountains that seem insurmountable or valleys you can't see your way out of. You may be searching for the next step in your journey, longing to go deeper in your relationship with Christ.

You may be so delirious with joy because of God's love for you and what He has done for you through Jesus Christ that you cannot wait to find a direction of service. No matter what your situation, your age, or your spiritual level, God wants to give you clearer vision.

CHAPTER 2

Charting Your Course

Can you imagine needing glasses to see and not even knowing it? Our friend Kim tells of when she was a teenager and was virtually blind in one eye but didn't realize it.

I wear glasses now and have worn them since tenth grade. Before then, I always thought I had excellent vision and never had reason to think I could not see. However, when I took the driver's education class my sophomore year in high school, they tested our eyes. While waiting my turn, I covered my eyes, and practiced the eye chart. To my dismay, the vision from my right eye was blurred and I could hardly see. I panicked—I could not fail this test. So I memorized the eye chart and when my turn came, I passed with flying colors!

When I got home, I told my parents about my eye problem. The ophthalmologist diagnosed me with a severe case of near-sightedness in my right eye.

My left eye was doing most of the work, and I have worn glasses ever since. I needed glasses not only to encourage my right eye to function better but to make my vision altogether clear.

Maybe you've had a time when your vision was blurred and glasses solved the problem. The writer of Proverbs talks about having a different type of vision, to which we referred in Chapter 1: "Where there is no vision, the people perish" (Proverbs 29:18 KJV). The writer of Proverbs is not talking about physical sight. Rather, he is talking about "spiritual" sight—a vision of hopes and dreams. Many women today have sight, but no clear vision for their lives.

"But what am I supposed to do?" Ginah asked. "I devoted my entire life to raising our daughter and now that she is on her own, I don't know what to do with my time. I haven't nurtured my talents or taken courses to improve my skills. I stayed at home to care for my family. Now Pete is traveling most of the week with his business. After I finish the housework in the morning, I feel so lonely and empty that I usually nap and watch television until he gets home for dinner."

Ginah is not alone. In the past five years, we have talked to Christian women across the nation—stay-at-home moms and career women, single and married women—and most were in agreement with Ginah that when you've denied your own needs and devoted so many years to nurturing others, it's not easy to focus on God's vision for your life.

We've been there. Maybe our vision was blurred

because we were so tired trying to balance babies and bylines! Nonetheless, we write from our hearts and are concerned that millions of women today have blurred vision. We know that amidst the dishes, diapers, PTA meetings, Sunday school classes, church committees, piano lessons, football games, business associates, and more, life is so chaotic that it's easy to lose focus. We know how natural it is to slip into a mundane existence filled with routine and busy-ness, doing so much for others until you finally burn out. Sometimes it feels more comfortable to "hide" behind our children, our husbands, or our careers than to stand strong as a unique child of God.

There is a better way. As you continue to read this book, we will help you evaluate your vision and target your unique gifts and personal calling. We challenge you to consider your passion—that highest vision in life—as you focus on reaching out and making a personal difference in the world, as well as fulfilling your own needs as a Christian woman. In doing so, we pray that you can:

- Discover God's call for your life.

- Discover the unique attributes and gifts God has given to you.

- Discover how to use these gifts to touch the lives of those around you.

As we work with women of all ages, we particularly see a vague depression and a yearning for personal fulfillment among women ages 30+, especially stay-at-home moms as their children start school. Sadly, one middle-aged woman recently shared, "Well, my kids are in school, and I sit home day after day waiting for God to show me what He wants out of my life. So far, He hasn't shown me a thing. I still have no vision."

Before we talk about discovering God's vision for your life, let's review our definition of "women of vision." A woman of vision fixes her eyes upon Jesus, her Savior, who walked the way of the cross and has called her to follow where He leads.

We have identified key characteristics that are vital to women who want to be women of vision.

Purpose

I can do everything through Him who gives me strength. **Philippians 4:13**

A woman with vision has a definite purpose in life. But whose purpose is it—hers or God's? It needs to be God's, of course! As you read this book and hear personal stories of how other women pursued God's vision in their lives, you may feel the gentle nudge of the Holy Spirit. Give in to this heavenly tug! Ask yourself: Do I want God to get in step with me or am I going to be in step with God?

A Christian woman with vision understands that her ultimate purpose for being is grounded and rooted in Jesus Christ, living and loving as He did, and witnessing to people of God's intense love for them. Whether you run a business, baby-sit for a neighbor who works outside the home, are a compassionate friend, help seniors with daily tasks, or tutor a special-needs child, God will use you to touch the lives of others.

Passion

"God has not called me to be successful; He has called me to be faithful." Mother Teresa

A Christian woman with vision understands that her purpose is to live a godly life. Women with vision also have passion—for their family and friends, for their spiritual gifts, for their unique talents, for those who do not know Jesus Christ as their Lord and Savior, and for people who are trying to live their lives outside God's love.

Ask yourself: What is the burning passion of my life? What is it that I would die for? What is it that would make me draw the line and say, "Here I stand"? What is it that I think about every day?

No one can deny the passion Mother Teresa had for the poor of India. What if that same kind of passion infected every Christian woman in our nation? In our world? What if we had this same kind of passion to touch the lives of those in our families, our neighborhood, our community—the ones who are not "lovely"? What if we had the same passion to use our unique gifts to touch lives?

As you reach outside yourself and keep your focus on Christ, those around you will become what *you* are. This means that if you are loving, forgiving, caring, giving, and compassionate, your family members, friends, coworkers, and acquaintances are likely also to be loving, forgiving, caring, giving, and compassionate.

A friend shared that she could not get along with a coworker who was constantly negative and sarcastic. "I could not mention the weather without a negative remark from this woman in my office," Lynn said. "I mentioned this to my pastor who suggested that instead of trying to change the woman, I should pray for her—so I did. I found it revealing that within a week, I noticed a subtle change in her behavior—she was friendlier, more receptive to a positive conversation with me. Soon we were eating lunch together and sharing pictures of our children. I found out that her husband had left her when she was pregnant and I invited her to our church. I realized God has the power to change any situation—but I had to change my reaction to those around me. It was truly a God moment!"

Power and Prayer

I sought the LORD, and He answered me, and delivered me from all my fears. Psalm 34:4 RSV

A Christian woman with vision has a powerful tool—prayer. No matter how much money you have or how strong you think you are, you cannot pursue clear vision on your own. Instead, pursue Christ. He will use the gifts He has given you and will show you His plan for you. Deb tells a story of when she began to pursue full-time writing, using her gifts.

> *I've always appreciated my gift of writing. Because of this gift, when our children were small, I was able to stay home with them, helping to support our family by writing freelance articles for women's magazines. I would get up at 4:00 A.M. each day, and work until the children*

awoke. Then at naptime, the three children would go to their rooms, and I would finish my articles and do the mailings.

When our oldest son began to look at colleges about seven years ago, we didn't know how we were going to cover the cost. Having worked as a freelance writer at home while raising children, my income was modest. While we could cover the cost of a state school in our city, Rob had his heart set on an excellent Ivy League school in the south. He was awarded a leadership scholarship to the college—if only we could come up with the rest.

After going over our already stretched budget, Bob and I knew that if Rob was going to realize his dream, I would have to write more. I had no problem writing more, I just needed the opportunity, and I did not know where to look.

I still remember praying to God that night. Rather than asking for gifts of money to pay the tuition, I said, "God, I'm so willing to use my writing talent to glorify Your name. If You will help me find opportunity, I will glorify Your name with the written word." I did not mind working hard, but for freelance writers, the window of opportunity often can be narrow.

Exactly one week later, after asking God to guide me toward more work, I received a phone call from a literary agent in New York. She had seen several of my health books at a bookstore in Manhattan and asked if I would consider ghostwriting a book for two Ph.D. dietitians. I was taken aback as it seemed so sudden and overwhelming—I mean, does God work this fast in our lives? Absolutely!

I took on that book project, then another and another. Since that day seven years ago, I have authored or co-authored a total of 40 books that can be found in bookstores around the country and on the Internet—many are translated in foreign languages. Not only did Rob go to the college of his dreams and on to graduate school, but our daughters, Brittnye and Ashley, were able to follow in his footsteps and attend the same college, receiving an excellent higher education.

I often wonder how my life would have been different if I had not asked God to guide me in using my talent, if I had continued to try to do it on my own. I now realize that it was not my vision to pour myself into writing books on health and relationships, it was God's. There is no way that I could have accomplished what I did without the hand of God touching me; nudging me when I suffered with writer's block; helping me feel rested when the alarm went off at 4:00 A.M. and deadlines were approaching; energizing me when my family's needs had to be met after putting in long days writing. I didn't write 40 books alone. I was merely the vessel God used to share a healing message with others.

(An added note: Because of the many books I wrote, in 1998 I was chosen by my alma mater, the University of South Florida, as the Outstanding Alumnus of the Year for contributions to journalism. Again, all glory goes to God.)

As you ask God to show you His plan or purpose in your life, it's important to remember that you cannot make the plan happen on your own. It is only by the power of the Holy Spirit. We can't do anything on our own strength. We need the indwelling power and presence of the Holy Spirit. Remember, we are not the source, we are only the instruments. We've got to be open to opportunities, as Deb shared, and we've got to be willing to be used by God. Until we trust Him, we won't be able to see what God can do.

Some women are guilty of thinking too small. After we explained how vital it is for women to have clear vision, our friend Sheila said, "The best I can do is to get up and get the kids off to school. There's no way I would have the energy to do much else each day."

Sheila's vision is probably not all it could be. While limiting her abilities, she also limited the myriad blessings we experience when we "let go and let God." Christian women with vision dream about possibilities that only happen with God. A woman with vision is a woman who depends entirely upon the Holy Spirit to live for today and for tomorrow, not in the past.

People

Brothers, think of what you were when you were called. Not many of you were wise by human standards; not many were influential; not many were of noble birth. But God chose the foolish things of the world to shame the wise; God chose the weak things of the world to shame the strong. ... It is because of Him that you are in Christ Jesus, who has become for us wisdom from God—that is, our righteousness, holiness and redemption. 1 Corinthians 1:26–27, 30

Christian women with vision know their purpose in life. They have passion, they have power, and they pray. But they also involve people in their vision, for what is love unless it is given away? We are here for the sake of people. We are here to share the Good News that God so loved the world that He sent His only Son, Jesus, to die for us all.

Jewel, a retired widow, spends her mornings making phone calls to invalids in her church. Once a week she takes baked goods and favorite inspirational books to other women in her neighborhood who are infirm, and she is motivated by the warm feelings she receives from these people. She is living proof that you don't have to win a Nobel Prize to be used by God!

Oliver Wendall Holmes said, "Every calling is great when greatly pursued." Consider the hundreds of people in your own neighborhood who do not know that God loves them. Have you called upon them? What about the thousands in your hometown or millions in your state? Have you worked through your church to share God's love with others? As Christian women, we are to greatly pursue sharing the Good News! We are called to wrap our arms around the people in our families, communities, and world, and to see these people with new eyes.

Christian women with vision have God in control of their lives. At a recent day-long seminar, Deb noticed a woman who appeared to be taking notes the entire seminar:

At first I was flattered that she was so interested in what I had to say. She had the seminar packet that contained an outline and about 10 articles on each of the topics, and was writing on the pages as I spoke. At the end of the seminar, she brought me the packet and as I opened it, I noticed that she had circled all the typographical errors! I nearly cried. Not because of the mistakes, but because this woman missed the point entirely.

Are you busy critiquing others, finding the typos of life? Or are you actively focused on Christ and willing to touch the lives of other people? You get out of life what you put into it. If you come expecting nothing, you will receive nothing. If you spend your days being critical of others and finding their faults (or typographical errors!), you will receive nothing in return. If you spend your days as Ginah did, feeling lonely, napping and watching television, again, you will receive nothing. If you don't put anything in, you won't get anything out.

Persistence

They devoted themselves to the apostles' teaching and to the fellowship, to the breaking of bread and to prayer. Acts 2:42

Persistence goes hand in hand with commitment. Persistence involves loyalty to what you know is true rather than what you might feel at a low moment. You don't use your talent by staying in your comfort zone! You sit at the computer, your design board, your lesson plans, the medical journals, or your Bible for hours on end, long after everyone else has quit. That's what it means in a secular sense to deny yourself and take up your cross. And this type of persistence is effective!

A large university conducted a study of leading artists, athletes, and scholars. The research was based on anonymous interviews with the top performers in various fields. These people included concert pianists, Olympic athletes, tennis players, sculptors, mathematicians, and neurologists. The researchers probed for clues as to how these achievers developed. For a more complete picture, they interviewed their families and teachers.

The report stated conclusively that drive and determination, not great natural talent, led to the extraordinary success of these individuals. While the researchers expected to find tales of great natural gifts, they didn't find any at all. The mothers interviewed often said it was another child in the family who had the greater talents.

The researchers found extraordinary accounts of hard work, dedication, and persistence. In another study, when the nation's top achievers were asked to rate the factors they consider most important in contributing to their success, persistence and hard work emerged as the highest-rated factors. Not talent, not luck, but persistence and hard work!

The secret is not only in working hard, but in working hard at godly things. In other words, to deny yourself and take up your cross doesn't necessarily mean to be a go-getter—but to be a go-giver. Being a woman of vision doesn't mean winning the rat race, but serving the human race in Jesus' name. That's the kind of self-denial and cross-bearing Christians are called to do.

Dream Dreams

Before you can have clearer vision, you must first acknowledge your worth as a woman and person. Although we will go further into targeting your special gifts in the next six chapters, right now we want you to affirm your amazing uniqueness and worth.

A popular magazine ran a fascinating article several years ago about men and women who make their living making extraordinary use of their natural senses. The article cited the practiced eye of a diamond inspector, the sense of feel of a wool inspector, the developed ear of a cymbal tester, the sense of smell of a fresh fish inspector, and the sense of taste of a milk taster. All acknowledged that they had no special gift in the area of their senses. They had simply trained themselves to use what they had to a high degree.

As Christian women, we are part of the unique body of Christ. We have various interests, talents, and skills. But because God created us all in His image as unique individuals, there is a niche for everyone. None of us has the same fingerprints or footprints. Did you know that each of us even has our own tongue print? Yes, at the basic level of our existence, we are all unique.

In the New Testament, Paul writes, "Having gifts that differ according to the grace given to us, let us use them: if prophecy, in proportion to our faith; if service, in our serving; he who teaches, in his teaching; he who exhorts, in his exhortation; he who contributes, in liberality; he who gives aid, with zeal; he who does acts of mercy, with cheerfulness" (Romans 12:6–8 RSV).

"Cheerfulness?" Ruth said. "I try to be cheerful when I wake up in the morning. After my quiet time of prayer, I am so filled with God's peace. Yet by the end of the day when my three kids are all pulling at me, the dogs are barking, and the phone is ringing off the hook, I'm as far away from being cheerful as one could be!"

As we shared with Ruth, while you may watch a television show and think that your life will never be perfect, it's important to realize that we live in the real world. Christian women with vision sometimes have difficulty getting along, making their children mind, and keeping busy schedules without getting stressed out. These women come in all shapes and sizes; they lose their temper, say things they don't really mean, and hold outrageous expectations for themselves and those they love. And even though they know the biblical promise we have of being gifted, they are still guilty of saying the following:

- I will never be good enough.
- I will never be able to pray like her.
- I will never be a good friend (or wife, mother, or daughter).
- I will never be able to make my kids happy.
- I will never be a risk-taker.

And the list goes on. If you are a conscientious woman, feelings of inadequacy abound. Yet to break the pattern of negative self-abuse, it is important to recognize the very things you do right and affirm them. Women who are perfectionists have a difficult time when anything in their "perfect" life plan goes wrong. And, if you have children, you know that things do go wrong as change, interruptions, and mishaps seem to go hand in hand with raising kids.

Self-respect is important as you seek God's clear vision—to feel the love and freedom that Christ Jesus can give. To respect yourself, you must acknowledge your giftedness—even when other parts of your life seem dismal. Through our Baptism, we are washed clean from the sin, guilt, and inadequacies of our sinful nature. We are new beings in Christ Jesus. Use this next section to remind yourself that you are God's child—a child He loves dearly.

Start with Affirmation

Using the list on page 50, write down your personal attributes in the five given spaces. These are the very strengths that make you special. Perhaps you pride yourself in being a compassionate wife, mother, and friend. Maybe you are an excellent friend and listener or have as much patience as Job. Or maybe you are tenacious and persistent, helping your family stay on a budget or meet a long-term goal.

Even if your greatest strength is waking your child up each day, fixing food for him, and making sure he gets on the school bus and does his homework at night, write it down. This is being steadfast! For many women, this would be quite an accomplishment, and you are to be affirmed.

Personal Attributes

Affirming	Compassionate	Conscientious
Dependable	Determined	Empathetic
Energetic	Enthusiastic	Ethical
Faithful	Friend	Honest
Listener	Loyal	Patient
Persistent	Reliable	Responsible
Spiritual	Steadfast	Trustworthy

My Personal Attributes as a Christian Woman

1. _____

2. _____

3. _____

4. _____

5. _____

You Are Loved Just Because

Turn to this page and review these unique attributes every morning during your quiet time with God. Thank Him for these special gifts. Whenever you have self-doubts, look at these personal attributes again. Say them aloud. Believe you have worth because God gave you these strengths.

When we build on our strengths as Christian women, we can begin to accept areas in our life over which we have no control. Isn't that a strength in itself—to accept and cope with our burdens and weaknesses? Personal weaknesses that used to haunt us with guilt are diminished when we thank God for our giftedness and ask Him to walk beside us each day.

As you read the next six chapters, remember that no one has written your script for you. It's perfectly all right if you forget your lines once in awhile because God has given you a learning laboratory to keep working at it—your home. God has also given you a clean slate to start over every day— His grace and forgiveness, ours through His Son, Jesus Christ. In that regard, be open to identifying your stumbling blocks in life—no time, too many commitments, misplaced priorities, or too much clutter—then begin to think about how you can get your life in order as you seek God's vision.

Cling to the Promise of Scripture

What is it that God has called you to do? Most of us had grand dreams and goals as young girls, yet how many actually see these dreams to completion? No matter what your home life is like, no matter how many work commitments you have, no matter what baggage you bring with you on your spiritual journey, God can clear up your blurred vision. Remember the promise in Job 14:7, "At least there is hope for a tree: If it is cut down, it will sprout again, and its new shoots will not fail."

Knowing that promise of hope can free you to launch out in faith—no matter what your situation in life—as you lean on your heavenly Father and the grace and forgiveness Jesus has won for you.

PART TWO:
Making the Connection

CHAPTER 3

Women with Vision Have Faith:

Connect Spiritually

Claire, an attractive middle-aged woman, lingered behind after a recent seminar, waiting to learn more about God's vision. We talked for a minute about her faith history and involvement in her church, then asked about her marriage, family, career options, hobbies, and activities.

Her story was one we hear frequently:

- Stopped education or career to raise a family
- Works part-time for extra money but not using her gifts
- Actively involved in her local church and community
- Little personal time for God and prayer
- Not enough meaningful experiences now that her children are gone

Claire acknowledged something that we all need to take seriously: "In trying so hard to raise our family while my husband, Richard, made a living, I've neglected to make a life."

"I feel so alone," she said, "now that the children are gone. Richard is so contented with his business, yet he does not seem to understand that I need something more."

Aren't we all like that at some point? Our vision is blurred and we don't even realize it until we can't see at all. We get so caught up in the pressures and busy-ness of rearing children and making financial ends meet that the only measurement we have of personal fulfillment lies in how much "stuff" we have acquired or the destination of our next summer vacation. In our free time we spend hours staring at the television soap operas or sitcoms or burying our heads in mass-market novels. So how do we clear up our blurry vision? We don't—Jesus does! Read on!

Stopping the Rat Race

"On your mark ... get set ... go!" That's how Lorri describes a typical day—from the moment the alarm startles her at 5:30 A.M., until her youngest child is tucked in bed for the night, and she passes out with exhaustion—her life is an interminable race. The problem is that in the midst of running faster and harder each day to meet new clients, take care of her family's needs, or volunteer at school or in the community, this 40-year-old mother and freelance journalist feels as if she never reaches the finish line.

"I think my nonstop life hit me the hardest when my 11-year-old son, Ben, bought two gerbils. One gerbil stayed in the corner of the cage quietly eating his food, while the other gerbil ran constantly on the metal wheel connected to the cage. Ben couldn't stop laughing at the hyperactive gerbil, going around and around, getting nowhere. I was laughing too, until my son said it reminded him of me."

There are times when most of us can identify with Lorri. We try to juggle all the responsibilities in life—kids, commitments, careers, and caregiving—but in the midst of our struggle to succeed or win in each area, we feel as if we are on a continuous treadmill stuck on high with no "off" button.

Oh, yes, we have it so good ... or do we? Women can do anything—or we can do everything! Yet a society infatuated with material success and results offers no solace to the harried. In the midst of our struggle for fulfillment, so many of us miss what is most important in life—spiritual wholeness and the clear vision only God provides.

You are probably well aware of the anguish caused by separating yourself temporarily from God because of your nonstop "busy-ness." Perhaps you have blamed your lack of purpose on the frantic pace of your life. But if your spirit is wrought by turmoil, when life's stressors hit, the pressure is magnified and it seems impossible to rejuvenate yourself after doing daily battle in today's world. As 45-year-old Patsy told us when her only child went away to college and she experienced the death of her mother and sister—all within a three-month period, "I went from feelings of anger, sadness, and loneliness ultimately to burnout."

Patsy continued, "After my mother died, my sister was killed in a work-related accident just one month later. I desperately needed consolation and comfort, but I didn't know where to turn."

Discovering Spiritual Strength

Over the past two decades, we have talked with hundreds of women of all ages who have sought guidance in finding God's purpose for their lives. Their stories are similar in that one of the main struggles most women face is years of ignoring their personal relationship with God through Jesus Christ. This intimate relationship fills the soul. It's that fulfillment that many women are missing.

Most women we have spoken to are dissatisfied with mundane career choices or the emptiness and lack of meaning in their daily lives, especially as their children grow more independent. Many have low self-esteem from years of abuse as children or as spouses. Others are simply burned out and too tired to care about the direction their lives are heading. But we have experienced that those women who have a deep sense of spirituality and listen to God's direction in their lives view life and love with a great sense of anticipation and hope.

A New Millennium Brings Change

It's a new millennium—a time when many women are coming to grips with their own mortality—we will not live forever. We have been loving daughters, wives, mothers, and friends; are ambitious in our careers and community involvement; are well educated and have material success. So why do many of us experience a void or loneliness and want to find answers for this nagging lack of purpose and inner peace?

It has happened to everyone. After an unusually tormenting day of trying to meet the needs of many, you stop right where you are and wonder, "Why am I doing this?"

Perhaps this "awakening" happened when you were hurrying your children to grab their backpacks so you could take them to school and still make that important breakfast meeting with your client. Maybe this occurred when you were doing some last-minute shopping after picking your children up from day care, trying to get through the checkout line as they pleaded for another favorite candy or toy. Whenever your awakening took place, did this moment motivate you to search for a new perspective on life?

Women who have been able to pursue higher education and career advancement should be satisfied, right? But we're not. In an era that has access to the latest medical advances and technology, we should feel healthy and vibrant. We usually don't. And as we come home to life in suburbia with late-model cars, VCRs, color TVs, surround-sound stereos, CDs, IRAs, and stock portfolios, we should be contented and secure. Maybe we're not.

One must wonder, if our lives appear so captivating— so together—why are so many of us experiencing the distressing anxiety of wanting something more?

Because we're missing the key ingredient in our lives: Jesus Christ. Only He can clear up your blurred vision and provide that "something more" you are seeking. He loves you like no other.

It is certainly no news to you that most of us are driven. We are driven to acquire; driven to achieve; and driven to success. However, this drive is taking its toll, resulting in tremendous stress and guilt for millions.

Sadly, while physicians used to say that 35 to 40 percent of the health problems Americans faced were stress induced, newer studies now indicate that stress could be responsible for as much as 60 to 80 percent of all physical problems. These stress-related disorders include headaches, high blood pressure, insomnia, back pain, muscle aches, as well as a host of psychiatric disorders.

The Quest for Inner Peace

If it isn't insomnia or a perpetual headache due to stressful living, most of us live with a constant nagging feeling that something is missing in life, a feeling that we liken to "soul sickness." In *Care of the Soul* (Harper Collins, 1992), Thomas Moore maintains that the soul has to do with genuineness and depth, as when we say certain music has "soul" or a remarkable person is "soulful." *Soul* is linked to life in all its particulars—soothing hymns, satisfying conversations, genuine friends, and experiences that stay in the memory and touch the heart.

When you are in touch with your soul and take daily responsibility for nurturing your relationship with God through Jesus Christ, all other areas of life, including clearing up that blurred vision, inevitably fall into place.

We know personally how easy it is to become overwhelmed with the stresses of today's society, but taking time to nurture your spiritual relationship with God is the basis for a Christ-centered life. For the past 20 years we have worked with women in the local church, community, and at seminars who sought guidance. We have found that the main struggle women have in understanding what God would have them do comes not from years of failed attempts at relationships, careers, volunteering, or trendy activities. Rather, it comes from years of ignoring their relationship with Jesus Christ. Women today tell of having unstable relationships and troubled families. Many have low self-esteem from years of abuse as children, while others are recovering alcoholics or children of alcoholics. Most are dissatisfied with their jobs and their daily lives. After counseling these women for years, we have found that most have neglected their souls and feel emotionally empty.

When we care for our souls and nurture our spiritual lives, all other areas of life inevitably fall into place. And this care of the soul means giving meticulous attention to our daily actions—what we listen to, what we feel, what we think, whom we befriend, what we read, and how much time we spend talking with God.

For millions of women today, life is confused, disorganized, frustrating, and, to be honest, quite difficult. For those women who, in the midst of making a living have ignored to make a life, listening to God's direction will inspire you to go on a multidimensional spiritual walk with our Lord that will enable you to feel a deeper sense of purpose and Christian wholeness. This faith walk means we must set our eyes on the cross of Christ and go toward this goal in all we do and say.

Inner Renewal

Genuine spirituality requires inner renewal rather than outward conformity. Therefore, strengthening your inner self will enable you to cope with life in a nondestructive manner. And nourishing your inner spirit involves pursuing a dynamic, forward-looking relationship with God through Jesus Christ.

A young mother at one of our seminars told us that she had recently become a Christian. We rejoiced with this woman as she had been struggling for several years. After she told us about her new life with Christ, she seemed confused, saying, "I know that I am a Christian in my mind, but how am I supposed to live? Does this change me in any way?"

To begin with, acknowledging that you are a Christian and learning to live in a Christlike manner are two separate matters. Being a Christian is a gift that is ours through the Holy Spirit working faith in us. We are brought to the throne of grace and forgiveness by the saving blood of Jesus Christ. It is a gift and we can do nothing to earn it. But to grow in this faith, we make time every day for personal devotion and study. This includes Bible study, prayer, meditation, personal reflection, and listening to God. And you can only do this if you make spiritual discipline a priority in your home.

Discipline comes from a word that has the same Latin root as disciple, which means to "teach and guide." Most women understand the biblical mandate to take control in the home by "disciplining" our children. We also know the importance of being disciplined in our lifestyle habits—eating right, exercising regularly, and getting restful sleep. But did you know that we are to be disciplined in our spiritual lives as well?

A daily spiritual time with God is a discipline that will enrich your life—both now and for years to come. As you start a devotional habit of Bible study, memorization of key verses, understanding Scripture, and developing a prayer relationship with God, you will be strengthened and upheld, even in times of crises, doubt, insecurity, or self-doubt. Remember Paul's words about this strength: "I can do everything through Him who gives me strength" (Philippians 4:13).

A personal faith in Jesus Christ gives ultimate purpose in life. Faith in Christ means that we have access to One who knows us best and loves us most. His love is so awesome that He gifted each of us with talents to make a difference in the lives of others. When we pursue knowing God through a faith relationship in Christ, we discover who we are and whose we are—the very reasons we were created.

Yet somehow the Christian faith is seen by many as a compliant lifestyle in which believers are reserved, submissive people who never venture out, never trouble the waters, and subsequently, never achieve great things. But the reverse is true: the Christian faith frees us to celebrate dynamic, forward-looking relationships with God. If you look at women with vision who are doers in your community, achievers in their careers, and who are enlarging their horizons with relationships with others, many of these women have a strong faith in God.

Take Time for Soul Food

Strengthening her faith through daily quiet times, prayer, Bible study, and fellowship, any woman can grow to better understand God's work in her life. She can know herself to be loved for who she is, not for what she does, how much money she makes, or how perfect she or her children appear to others. How can you nourish your faith?

Start by building your personal identity. Before you can understand God's direction for you, it's important to know and understand who you are and to really love that person. Then you can better decide where you want to go—and how to get there.

Studies reveal that people who are anchored with a strong faith and a spiritual base feel more secure and have higher self-esteem. Self-worth is not dependent on external forces, but on a strong internal drive that lets us value who we are without a codependent need for approval from others. As you nurture your faith, you will boost your self-esteem so that spiritual connection with God and others becomes a reality.

If your self-esteem is low, it is not too late to nurture it. Here are some symptoms of low self-esteem in adults as well as ways to improve it.

Symptoms of Low Self-Esteem

- Often feeling jealous or insecure in relationships
- Having difficulty giving or accepting compliments
- Not knowing what you want—from dinner choices to career goals
- Knowing what you want but not asking for it—in relationships, at work, or at home
- Rarely expressing your feelings—whether anger, sadness, or love
- Blaming others for your dissatisfaction or unhappiness

Take time out. Once you've identified symptoms of low self-esteem, you can take time to nurture yourself by yourself. The Bible has a wealth of insight into the need to be alone. Being alone, as indicated by the life of Jesus, need not be a time for feeling lonely—we can feel lonely in the midst of a crowd. Being alone can be a time for finding meaning in your life. When Jesus was in solitude, He found His source of power. After spending the day preaching to and teaching the vast crowds, He "went up on the mountain by Himself to pray" (Matthew 14:23, RSV). Luke told of Jesus spending time teaching and nurturing the people, then He "withdrew to the wilderness and prayed" (Luke 5:16, RSV).

Often we can become so saturated with church meetings, school commitments, and community obligations that we experience a spiritual void. During these busy times our thoughts often become disorganized, and our relationships with our spouses can seem stifled. This turmoil usually occurs because we did not take time for renewal or to get our priorities in order while we were in solitude.

Elizabeth agreed that taking time to be alone—without her husband Steve—was vital as she sought something more in her life. Why? Because in order to be intimate with someone else, you must first celebrate who you are. Alone time is the perfect time for renewal and self-discovery. "When you are in solitude, you can discover what you love most, what makes you feel alive, relaxed, and complete," Elizabeth shared. "During these times of solitude, you can pray, meditate, read the Bible and inspirational books; walk alone on the beach, relax in a hot bath, or set personal goals and be at one with God. It's wonderful to be alone each day because you make a more complete partner for your spouse.

Keep a spiritual journal. To "see clearly," you must do some intimate homework, plotting your spiritual journey and observing times where God is trying to get your attention. This can be done with a journal—a lined, ringed-notebook that can be purchased at any drugstore, grocery store, or bookstore. A personal journal can help you uncover your inner self. Each day you can assess your emotional attitude, learn how the highs and lows of contemporary life affect you and your relationships, and witness how God is moving in your life. This confessional writing will capture your deepest feelings—thoughts that you might not feel comfortable sharing aloud. With the journal, you can look back after several weeks and examine your faith and relationships at their highs and lows, peaks and valleys. The journal can also become an intimate place where you can ventilate, meditate, problem solve, and dream—without feeling threatened or intimidated. We use spiritual journals to keep prayer lists, write down answers to prayers, and set goals.

We have found opening up our imagination and reflecting deeply about our spiritual life is important. This means counting our daily blessings and writing them down; naming a moment of happiness and recording it; and getting in touch with our spirit as we become more aware of God working in us.

Do a periodic attitude check. Trying to be all things to all people is nothing new for most women today. But struggling to please everyone can often affect our emotional state, causing temper flares or impatience. It is helpful to come to terms with any negative attitudes and behaviors before they become hurtful. When you take your periodic timeouts during the day, do an attitude check, then briefly write your feelings in a journal. Look back over your journal entries after several days or weeks, and see the ups and downs of your emotions. Can you see God working through you and the resulting attitude toward others? Reflect from time to time on these journal entries to see how God is moving in your life.

Spend time in prayer. Prayer continues that personal relationship with God that most long for, and it helps to switch your body into a calmer, more peaceful mood. Prayer helps you regain a sense of peace when daily stressors create anxiety and tension. It also allows you time to refocus your attention on God and His plan for your life. Make sure you have a regular time to pray to God each day. But don't limit yourself to just that regular time. As Paul told the Thessalonians, "Pray without ceasing" (1 Thessalonians 5:17 KJV).

Spend time listening to God. This doesn't mean asking God for answers. Rather, it means asking what questions God has for you. How can God speak to us during these times of spiritual renewal? This is where Christian risk is involved—to be willing to sort through messages and launch out on the ones we feel are of God. The more aware we become of God's presence during alone times through contemplative listening, through Scripture, and through study, the more "real" God becomes to us. A communication is at work; a relationship grows—a relationship which was sealed in our Baptism.

Suggestions for alone time:

- Read Scripture; memorize key verses (see John 6:15; Luke 22:41; Luke 9:18; Mark 1:35).
- Take a home study course—on books in the Bible or a study of Christian beliefs.
- Go for a nature walk and marvel at God's creation.
- Learn a new talent or skill, such as sewing, painting, or playing the piano.
- Keep prayer lists; study the meaning of prayer.
- Chart your personal and spiritual goals for the day, week, and month.
- Read inspirational books or poetry.
- Read a book by a favorite author.
- Do creative writing for personal pleasure.
- Write letters to friends; write letters to enemies asking for forgiveness.

Focus spiritually with ongoing personal and family devotions. Slow down an hour before bedtime, and encourage family members to do the same. Turn off the television and spend this downtime reading your Bible or a devotional book. If you have children at home, read together from such devotional books as *Little Visits with God* (Concordia, 1995) or *Laugh and Tickle, Hug and Pray* (Concordia, 1997). Play a tape of restful hymns or contemporary Christian music by artists such as Point of Grace or Michael W. Smith, and think about the messages the words convey.

Study the Christian faith as taught in God's Word. The Bible is central to our understanding of the Christian faith—it teaches us God's plan for our lives as we see God's love in action. In 2 Timothy 3:16–17, we find that the Bible is God's tool, making us well-prepared at every point, fully equipped to do good to everyone. The Bible is divinely inspired by God and teaches us what is true—right and wrong. And while reading the Bible for inspiration is important for Christians, Bible *study* is necessary as we learn to apply Scripture to our daily lives. The Old Testament tells us about our heritage and the Law; the New Testament teaches us about Christ and the Gospel. Understanding the Scriptures, like being a Christian, is a lifelong process. The Bible was penned by about 40 men of many occupations. They wrote over a period of approximately 1,500 years, and in three languages—Hebrew, Aramaic, and Greek. The Bible consists of 66 books and is divided into two parts, the Old Testament and the New Testament (the word testament means covenant). Yet the Bible has one great theme and central figure—Jesus Christ—and one supreme author, the Holy Spirit.

Celebrate Sunday as our Lord's day. As you set your eyes on Christ, asking God to fix your blurred vision, pause one day a week for personal recovery, spiritual renewal, and family bonding. In the midst of the struggle to hurry and reach a career or financial goal or life destination, many of us realize that we must also balance the stress and busy-ness of our lives with a day of rest. Taking Sunday as a special day for recovery and renewal will add much-needed energy and meaning to your week. After a long week of intense, creative work, rest is in order. Taking time to read the funny papers, to have a leisurely breakfast with family members, to attend church as a family, then celebrating the afternoon with time together can help recharge you for the upcoming workweek.

Join a church, and celebrate weekly worship with other Christians. For most of us this time of worship each week is when we shift our burden from our shoulders to God's. We find our strength in the Word of the Lord, and we commune with our brothers and sisters in Christ. For this fellowship, church membership is important, and being in regular attendance is vital to spiritual discipline. This means actively involving yourself in the life of the church, including Sunday school, Bible studies, music programs, worship, and more. The church will enhance the spiritual journey you are now taking as it provides training in the Christian faith.

Share kindness with others. Love is not love until it is given away. Pause periodically throughout the day and do random acts of kindness for those around you. These are good deeds done for others when they least expect it. These random acts of kindness may involve a phone call, a note in the mail, a plate of homemade cookies, or fresh flowers from your garden. After you practice a few random acts, ask yourself: How did you feel doing this action? Did it surprise the recipient? Reflect on your insights and feelings, and challenge yourself to continue to do acts of kindness, sharing God's love and experiencing His greatest rewards.

Savor "God Moments." God is made known to us in every part of life—not just in daily quiet time or in a sermon or devotional booklet. How can you see God each day? His voice speaks to us when:

- We drive noisy carpools to school.
- The homeless person on the street cries for help.
- The neighbor next door drops in for coffee and really needs someone to confide in.
- The child gives us a hug just "because."
- Our husband or friend tenderly comforts us when we are sad.
- Our parent witnesses to God's love during a terminal illness.
- Our boss reconciles feuding workers.

Vision Requires Discipline

The more disciplined you are in nurturing your devotional habit—spending time regularly with God—the more aware you will become of God's vision for you. But it is not easy to establish spiritual disciplines today. It often seems that just when you sit down to read the Bible or pray, the phone rings loudly, there is a knock at the door, or a family member has a need—that only you can meet. Make it a priority to pause from the busy world and set aside daily alone time to develop a devotional habit. Commit your life to Jesus Christ, your Lord and Savior.

CHAPTER 4

Women with Vision Are Empowered:

Connect Personally

$\mathcal{W}$ith God, nothing is wasted.

People often ask us to speak to groups about writing. Ellen recently spoke to several groups of middle and high school English students.

I am challenged when I speak to youth, especially knowing how most kids feel about writing. Students conjure up two completely different ideas for the words "writer" and "writing." Often, they picture a writer as a famous recluse, wearing a floppy hat and sitting by the ocean writing romance novels. Or some envision a writer to be an eccentric who sits by the sea smoking a pipe, writing murder mysteries. Sometimes they picture writers living in Hollywood or New York.

I attempt to convince them that we are all writers. Just as I write books and articles, they write book reviews, essays, research papers, love letters, e-mails, and the dreaded thank-you notes. Even if they receive no payment or feel forced to write, they are still writers.

When most teenagers hear the word "write" or "writing," they do not hear the waves crashing at the beach in the background. They automatically conclude that they can never write well enough to be famous, so they decide they cannot write at all. The majority convince themselves they hate writing.

The teenagers I speak to always ask how I became a writer. Some ask about my college studies and what I chose for a major. My answer is not about learning from writing courses, but rather from a continuum of experiences. I tell students that my writing career began in elementary school as teachers gave grades in writing. My sixth-grade teacher set aside time every Friday for creative writing. During the week, we worked on a special writing project, and on Friday, we presented it to the class. We could write poetry, songs, stories, the weather report, news, or anything else we could imagine. I remember writing a cliff hanger series about a girl who lived in Idaho on her family's sweet potato farm. I so creatively named her "Yammy." Each week, Yammy faced a new peril that demanded brains and courage and the help of her trusted dog. Obviously, if I still remember this experience, it had a lasting impression.

My writing career continued in junior high school as teachers required more writing skills from students and in high school where I wrote speeches for elections and speech class, announcements for clubs, club minutes, and articles for the school newspaper.

When I was editor of the high school newspaper, I never dreamed I would one day be a magazine editor for six years. I never knew that speaking in church, organizing Sunday school parties, or participating in mission trips and mission projects would prepare me for all I would do in the future.

As I tell students, everything we do today prepares us for what we will do tomorrow. I didn't have to wait until I was an adult to learn to communicate; God began the training years before. My desire is to empower students to start learning now. As we look at the endless list of experiences that can lead to a writing career, I see their enthusiasm growing. They move beyond thinking that writing is just about books and writers are just about beaches. They gain new insight about the possibilities.

Having gifts that differ according to the grace given to us, let us use them. Romans 12:6 RSV

Catch the Vision

It takes all kinds of people to give us the multitude of written communication we have today. It takes all kinds of empowered women to share their gifts with their family, their church, their community, and a world in need. Students find it difficult to envision themselves as writers until they are given a new vision for writing. It is after they feel empowered that the enthusiasm comes and their eyes are opened to new possibilities. It is the same for you. Many women go about their day-to-day routines tending to countless details, but feel powerless, purposeless, and lonely. Perhaps you have tried to empower others when you have no strength left to feel empowered yourself.

Women have been led to believe that our role is to sacrificially take care of everyone else's needs. Let's look at what is wrong with that belief. You are only one person. There is no way you can take care of all the needs of all the other people in your life. You are not Superwoman.

Sometimes we live to sacrifice and take care of others so we continue to feel and be needed. The psychological term for this is co-dependency. You are depending on others to meet your needs for self worth. That is unfair to them and to you. Both of you will fail because at some point, they will not need you as much as you need to be needed or they will need you so much that you will burn out and no longer want to meet their needs. And where does that leave you? Where does it leave them? When you continuously sacrifice for others, you sacrifice yourself. You lose your own sense of self. You really don't know who you are or who God wants you to be apart from the other people you think you must take care of. The healthier perspective is to learn to care for others while teaching them to take care of themselves. The best way to do that is for them to see that you actually take time to care for yourself whether that is a quiet time with your Bible and God, exercise, or any special activity you enjoy. You can teach others that God expects us to be good stewards of what He has created us to be. Taking care of yourself and using your gifts in reasonable service is honoring God's gift to you. Learn to care for others, but let God take care of them too.

Join the "Women of Awakenings"

When we think of women who empowered others, we never cease to be amazed with the Old Testament story of Deborah. In their book, *Women of Awakenings*, authors Lewis and Betty Drummond refer to Deborah as "the only woman in the Old Testament elevated to a position of political and spiritual power by the common consent of the people. Few women in the history of the human race have ascended to the place of power, dignity, and authority among her people as did Deborah." [1]

Where did Deborah come from? We don't know all the details from Scripture, but it is obvious that God prepared her and she listened and responded to His call. Deborah was a housewife, living in the hill country of Ephraim. Her husband apparently had little prominence among the Israelites. God prepared this ordinary housewife for a significant role in history. She became recognized as a prophetess and judge. God used her boldness and obedience to help turn the heart of Israel. In collaboration with

Barak, one of Israel's key military leaders, Deborah assembled a huge army that ultimately defeated the Canaanites.

To think that a woman in the Middle East in Old Testament times was revered as a leader of a champion army is unbelievable. How could it happen? Deborah was obedient to answer God's call to service and leadership. God called her to make a difference in the spiritual condition of the nation of Israel. She could have been too scared, too intimidated, too emotional, or not willing to take a risk. Answering God's call is a risky process—a journey. You never know just where His call will take you, but He promises to go before you and to stay with you always.

God's Eye Chart

Novelist and preacher Frederick Buechner likes to think about life as an alphabet by which God makes His power and purpose known to us. Buechner compares God's alphabet of grace to the Hebrew alphabet, which has no vowels. Filling in the vowels is left to each of us as we interpret His grace. Unlike fixed words in a dictionary, God speaks to us in such a way that the spelling is different for each person. He loves us as individuals. He calls us as individuals. Let's look at some of the ABCs that will help improve your vision.

A Is for Attitude

You know the expression, "You are what you eat." We used to think that was just outward evidence that you were overeating. If you were overweight, then you didn't eat the right foods. Now, we know that some eating problems stem from what is going on inside us. One woman may look model-thin and be emotionally ill and anorexic. Another woman may be 50 pounds overweight because she eats to escape her problems. The same is true for what you think. You are what you think. Even if you keep what you think bottled up and never share your real thoughts or feelings with anyone, they still dominate your life. You might be spending much of your energy protecting your inner feelings and thoughts from others. Eventually, your thoughts will catch up with you and outwardly, often gradually, affect your lifestyle. Your thoughts control your attitudes toward life, other people, and yourself. If you continuously "feed" on negative thoughts about yourself and others, you will become a negative person. If you are raising children, chances are they will begin to see life through your negative eyes. In today's society, you must aim to be positive. From all avenues of society you hear negative messages. The media hungers for the negative and controversial. Politicians crave the negative in order to form defensive platforms. Some ministers raise the negative so we will find a more godly standard. If you want to stay realistic, but positive, you must work at it. Uplifting the negative takes very little energy, but to continue to be negative uses up much creative, loving energy. Pessimism and negativity block the possibility of clear vision.

What's Your A.Q.? (Attitude Quotient)

Finally, brothers, whatever is true, whatever is noble, whatever is right, whatever is pure, whatever is lovely, whatever is admirable—if anything is excellent or praiseworthy—think about such things. Philippians 4:8

Our motto is, "Find the silver lining." Nothing will ever be perfect, but that does not mean we have to stop ourselves from being grateful for something. Some call it an Attitude of Gratitude. What can you do to cultivate a positive attitude?

- Read books about hope and a positive attitude. Keep them near your bed or your desk. Underline important phrases so you can pick the book up and immediately gain strength from a familiar positive phrase.

- Write positive quotes and Scripture verses that give you strength on cards. Place a card in your car, on the refrigerator, your bedroom mirror, your bathroom mirror, or in your office drawer.

- Keep positive words and phrases before you as much as possible. Not only will they motivate you, they will give you the opportunity to tell others about your reason to be positive: you serve a God of hope, grace, and forgiveness.

- Choose your "whine time" carefully. Pick a trusted friend, family member, or coworker, and allow yourself a few minutes to talk about something that is troubling you. Sometimes the positive words of others and their hugs and prayers can help you "see better."

- When you must face something negative or discuss something negative with someone else, try to end the conversation on a positive note. What can you do to change the situation? If you cannot do anything, then vow to find positive outlets and move on. If you can change the situation to create a more positive environment or outcome, then set goals and priorities to proceed.

- At the end of every day or every week, ask God to help you reflect on all you have and all He has done for you. What are you grateful for? Even difficult situations can help us learn more about God, about ourselves, and about how to deal with others. What did you learn? How will you be different next week because of what you learned this week?

- Do one simple thing to bless someone else every day. Maybe it's a quick phone call to a friend to cheer her up. Maybe it's a note in your child's lunch box. Maybe it's a Hershey's Kiss on your husband's pillow. Maybe it's sending a card to a parent or relative. Don't make it hard or time consuming, just fun.

- Do one special thing a week that stretches your comfort zone. (If you are overwhelmed by problems or work right now, commit to once a month.) Take some brownies to a new neighbor. If you see that someone in your neighborhood just had a baby, put a Christian parenting magazine in their mailbox with a note of congratulations.

- Take a hurting friend to lunch.

- Focus on using positive words and phrases such as *hope, opportunity, I can, I will try,* and *possibility.* Avoid words and phrases such as *I can't do it, I will never, I don't know what to do,* or *I give up.*

Warning: Negative Person Sighted

Beware of negative people. It is all too easy to succumb to their pessimism and gossip. But it's like eating too many chocolate chip cookies at one time. The first bites are mouth watering, but after devouring more than the limit, you begin to feel sick and terribly guilty for consuming that many calories in one sitting! If you are trying to remain positive and are asking God to help you, know that if you stay around negativism for long periods, you will begin to feel sick and terribly guilty. Just as too much sugar sends your body into a high and then a tailspin that leaves you tired, negative talk and people zap you of needed energy. It takes focused energy to take care of yourself and follow your vision. Don't use it up on empty talk that only hurts others.

Our friend, Marilyn, tells of making a difficult friendship decision several years ago. She lived in a small town where gossip was a way of life. Every time her Sunday school class or garden group met together, the conversation centered much more around the town's latest divorce, cancer victim, or church problem than around God or flowers. Marilyn began to feel convicted that there had to be more to life than getting together for "hearsay sessions" about the crises in others' lives. She talked to her Sunday school teacher about it and they committed to pray for God to create a fresh spirit of hope and service among their class members. Marilyn suggested that instead of just praying for someone, that the class actually minister to the person in need. She noticed that the tendency was to use prayer request time as an excuse to catch up on church gossip.

As requests were made, a follow-up ministry action was suggested and a class member volunteered to make sure the action was completed. When a young girl in the church was going through a divorce, the class collected enough used furniture from their own attics and garages to furnish her apartment for her. When one member's teenage daughter became pregnant, Marilyn led the class to give her a baby shower and volunteer to provide free baby-sitting once a week so the girl could continue her college classes at night. The class found it hard to gossip if they were ministering to and truly praying for someone.

However, Marilyn did not have the same success with her garden group. She tried to suggest how the members could use gardening to better the community and help others, but the group was not willing to change their traditional meeting style. According to Marilyn, what they really were not willing to do was give up their gossip sessions and easy getaway times. So, Marilyn gave them up. She could no longer waste her time and energy on something that brought her down emotionally, physically, and spiritually. She wanted more and God gave it to her.

Discovering what it means to be a woman of vision may cause you to make some difficult decisions and choices. Look for positive ways to affect negative situations before you give up. If you cannot effect change, spend your energy on more productive things that motivate you to be the best you can be.

B Is for Baggage

If you have any encouragement from being united with Christ, if any comfort from His love, if any fellowship with the Spirit, if any tenderness and compassion, then make my joy complete by being like-minded, having the same love, being one in spirit and purpose. Do nothing out of selfish ambition or vain conceit, but in humility consider others better than yourselves. Each of you should look not only to your own interests, but also to the interests of others. Your attitude should be the same as that of Christ Jesus: Who, being in very nature God, did not consider equality with God something to be grasped, but made Himself nothing, taking the very nature of a servant, being made in human likeness. And being found in appearance as a man, He humbled Himself and became obedient to death—even death on a cross! **Philippians 2:1–5**

Many times our vision is clouded and our journey is hard because our load is too heavy. If you have flown very often, you know how cumbersome baggage can be. Airlines enforce strict rules about how much baggage you can store in overhead bins. Whether you take your baggage on the plane or check it at the ticket counter, it is still a pain to maneuver through airports with it.

Try this exercise: Hold onto a suitcase or big bag and see how many other things you can pick up and carry at the same time. Keep holding the bag and try to hug someone. No matter what you do, the suitcase is in the way. It is difficult to hold onto anything or anyone else with baggage taking up space. There could not be a more accurate picture of how many people drag through the journey. The emotional load of the past weighs them down and impacts everything they do.

Maybe you can identify with a young woman, Leslie, whom we met at a recent seminar. She knew she needed help. She constantly battled a poor self-image that kept her from enjoying life and her family. She thought that marriage would make her happy and children would bring even more happiness. Instead, Leslie felt that her husband and children simply used her. She felt that she was of no real value to anyone. A friend suggested she go talk to a Christian counselor. It did not take many sessions for the counselor to discern Leslie's self-worth problem dated back to her teen years. Leslie's 2-year-older sister was the beauty of the family. Leslie never felt as pretty or as valued for who she was as she thought her sister did. Her sister was homecoming queen and a cheerleader. Leslie received the math award at graduation and a great college scholarship, but at family gatherings, it was her sister who received the attention. Leslie's feelings about her sister and about herself weighed her down like a giant suitcase. She bumped into it every time she tried to do anything. She couldn't emotionally love her husband or her children in a healthy way because she couldn't love and accept herself. Leslie was actually passing her baggage on to her children. They could not get close to their mom because her emotional load was always in the way. Leslie's load was too heavy for her children to carry.

After months of counseling, much prayer, and honest talks with her husband, Leslie began to heal. She saw that she was made in the image of God and God compared her to no one. Gradually, she unpacked her suitcase and set it aside. For the first time she could remember, she was free to be herself. She was free to love and live as God made her. As a result, Leslie began to look for places where other women needed help. Her "new eyes" led her to a battered women's shelter where she started going once a week to assist with a support group. God used Leslie's own journey of pain to enable her to empathize with others.

So what can you do? Go directly to Baggage Check. Are you over the weight limit? Is your vision blurred because you are concentrating so hard on carrying your load? Now is the time to get help. Now is the time to unpack your bags and lighten your load for your sake, for your family's sake, for your friend's sake, and for the sake of those whose lives you can impact. Start by praying, asking your heavenly Father for forgiveness, and asking Him to help you empty your suitcase and put it away.

C Is for Connection

Once you have dealt with the emotional baggage from your past, you are free to find some healthy connection between your past, present, and future. It does not matter what events have transpired in your past or present, everyone longs for some connection to his or her historical self. Each one of us desires some sort of roots, something that gives us a foundation for who we are. It is as if our vision for the future must somehow be linked to our memory of the past. Our children long to know the little details about our past that give them some insight into who we were. Even if you would rather forget your past, stretch to find some details that you can share with others. In getting rid of your baggage, we challenged you to face your past head-on and realistically look at how it shaped your life. Now, we challenge you to look for some positive details that gave you strength.

- Who gave you support? A teacher, a minister, a parent, or a friend?
- What did you do for fun as a child? Remember your first bike, building forts, playing house, or fishing?
- When did you first start thinking about God? Did you hear about Him at church, from a parent, from a teacher?
- What spiritual events helped you strengthen your relationship with Christ?
- What did you enjoy the most? Television shows, books, music, or movies?
- Did you travel? What places do you remember the most?
- Was your town small or large? Where could kids go to have fun?
- Can you remember the people who hugged you? Your parents, grandparents, a teacher, or a church leader?
- What do you remember about your relatives? Did your grandmother's house have its own smell? What did you do when you visited your grandpa's farm? How crazy was your great-aunt?

Allow yourself to think about the past and evaluate the people and events that shaped your life. You will rediscover where your strength came from. You will remember whose love and care made a difference in how you felt about yourself. You will recall the people who invested their time in your life. You may have to weed through some difficult memories, some unpleasant people, and some painful events. But you will fit the pieces together and focus on a clearer picture of who you have been, who you are, and who you want to be. It is only after we begin to take the journey back through time that we can move forward through time.

Brio magazine, published by Focus on the Family, helps teenage girls understand who they are in Christ as they live in today's fast-paced society. In our interview, Editor Susie Shellenberger spoke fondly of the memories that shaped her life. "The greatest gift my parents gave me and the greatest gift any parent can give their daughter is a spiritual legacy. My parents would turn off the TV and have family prayer time. We talked about important issues. I knew what was non-negotiable with my parents, but I also knew I could go to them with anything I needed to. Every girl ought to have somebody she can go to. There should be no question she can't ask her mom, no matter how bad she thinks it might sound. And moms need to respond with honest, straight answers."

Susie is moved and challenged by the thousands of letters she gets from ordinary girls all over the world who are doing extraordinary things through their commitment to God, no matter the sacrifice. She continues to challenge teenage girls to take a sacrificial stand for God. Susie readily admits that part of the strength of who she is today came from the support and encouragement of her parents who loved her and believed in her. What's your story? Whatever it is, starting today, God wants to give you a clear picture of where you have been so you can help others know where they are going. He can use any event of your past to give you insight into the needs of others. He has been there all along and it is His desire to walk with you into the journey of the future.

D Is for Determination

Jesus Christ is the same yesterday and today and forever. Hebrews 13:8

Hang on. We are almost to the letter E. We have one more letter to reinforce, and it is vitally important to the alphabet of your journey. There is no way to get to E without going through the letter D for determination. A contemporary shoe commercial would say, "Just Do It!" If you want an idea of where God can use you, look for it. God is gracious to put people and events in your path along the way to encourage you and teach you. With determination, follow where He leads.

D is the letter at the crossroads. Determination moves you down the road. You decide that no matter what happens, you will keep on taking small steps even when your vision is dim and your path unsure. Some people make this decision once and for all. They determine there must be something more and they press on to discover what God wants to do in their lives. You may not be like them. You may come to a crossroads once a week or once a month, where you are forced to determine with new energy and courage to face the future.

Ellen is a walker. She understands the science of walking and the benefits to her health.

I love to walk. I try to walk three miles five times a week. When I walk, my mind leaps from one idea to another. I solve problems, create new books, discover new plants for my yard, meet people in my subdivision, and talk to God. It is a wonderfully freeing time. However, as much as I enjoy it, I have to make the decision to do it each time. I must re-determine each time that I need to walk. Once I start and get "down the road," I know I made the best choice and I vow that tomorrow I will not have to convince myself of its enjoyment and benefits again. But I do.

It would be easier if you could determine once and for all to do what God wants you to do. Ellen knows walking is good for her. She knows she feels better when she walks. But she still has to convince herself to walk each day. The same is true for us. We know what God would have us do, but we are sinful human beings and fall into temptation over and over. So how do we get the determination to get back up and try it all again? It is through the Holy Spirit, working determination in us, that we are able to do anything. With His leading, we continue on the journey set before us. For more on this struggle, read Romans 7:7–25.

E Is for Empowerment (Or All of the Above)

I can do everything through Him who gives me strength. **Philippians 4:13**

If you tried to jump right to E, we would have to mark your multiple-choice selection incorrect. You cannot conjure up empowerment—it's a process. Staying empowered requires a constant re-evaluation of where you want to go and what it takes to get there. We have already shared some practical steps to empowerment.

A—Attitude check

B—Baggage check

C—Connect the dots

D—Determine to do it

E—All of the above

We can't offer you a money-back guarantee on this list, but we will assure you that if you sincerely and prayerfully follow the A-B-C-D list, you will be well on your way to being empowered. You will know more about who you are in Christ. You will be freer to see the needs of others while still caring for yourself.

Becoming empowered is not an empty cry for feminism. Rather, it is an understanding that God wants you to be a whole creation, living an abundant life. When you are empowered in Christ, there is nothing to stop the unquenchable spiritual desire to live out this love adventure with Him. Complete the following exercise as a first step toward empowerment.

Empowerment Exercise

Complete the following sentences:

With God's help,

I will

_____.

I can

_____.

The future is

_____.

I have the potential to

_____.

I will look back and

_____.

Read through these sentences frequently. Your renewed sense of spiritual energy will give you enthusiasm for the journey. Your life cannot help but impact the lives of others.

CHAPTER 5

Women with Vision Are Resilient:

Connect Emotionally

Why are fairy tales so popular? It is certainly not because men have flocked to see the movie versions or read the books all these years. You know who usually buys the fairy tale books or videos for their children and grandchildren. Women love the "magic" of a happy ending. We pay good money for books and movies in which the plot involves a beautiful heroine overcoming the odds to find her fortune—and usually her prince. We dab our eyes and sigh as they ride off into the sunset. Perhaps we crave those endings so much because we know better. We know that life is not full of happy endings, no matter how much we wish upon a star. Unless we have overlooked a specialty shop somewhere, there is no magic wand.

As we searched through Scripture, we could not find a single verse where God promised that life would always be fun and easy. Real life is full of interruptions, transitions, and crises. Life does not move and has never moved on a level plane. We certainly have felt our own share of unhappiness, pain, and difficulties. If we could sit down with you right now and allow you to tell us about your experiences with real life, what would you say? What is your story?

Everyone has a story. Even the women who look like they have it all together have a story. Don't let them fool you. No matter how much money someone has, how beautiful she is, or how wonderful her husband and children might be, everyone has to deal with a crisis at some point in life.

Storytime Exercise

Pull out a piece of paper and a pencil and write out what you would share with us. What events and transitions have made life less than a fairy tale for you? Take time to list them.

Now, look over that list. Even if you are in the middle of a crisis right now, you are still alive. You are not only alive, you are reading a book about moving forward and becoming a woman of vision. You are a survivor. Whether it is a painful childhood, a devastating loss through death or divorce, financial setbacks, or just forgetting to celebrate yourself as a redeemed child of God, you have survived and are surviving. The Bible is full of testimonies of survivors, many of whom made costly mistakes, but God still used them for His purposes.

Scripture Survivors

Read the first six chapters of the Old Testament book of Joshua to recall how God used Rahab the Harlot to protect the Israelite spies. Rahab risked her life to save theirs. Many scholars believe it is the same Rahab who is listed as the mother of Boaz in the lineage of David. And it is from the lineage of David that we trace the birth of Christ. Only a God who loves us unconditionally would choose to use a prostitute in the grand scheme of redemption.

God Affirms the Woman at the Well

Look in John chapter 4 to see how God used the Samaritan woman at the well to reveal more of the deity of Christ to the world. Despite the past, her excitement over meeting the man who knew everything she had ever done caused many other Samaritans to believe in Jesus. God made something beautiful out of her broken life and used her honesty and boldness.

God Answers Hannah's Prayers

God answered the prayers of Hannah and gave her a son. She remained faithful to God and gave her son Samuel back to God to be used as a helper to the priest, Eli. Read in 1 Samuel, chapters 1 and 2 how Hannah visited her son once a year and brought him clothes she made especially for him. We often talk about Hannah's dedication to keep her promise to God, but we seldom talk about how hard it must have been for her to leave her young son with Eli and walk away, knowing she would only see him once a year. She would not see him learn to climb a tree, or run a race, or carry oil for the temple lamps. It must have taken extreme courage for her to honor her pledge to God.

God Chooses Mary to Bear the Christ Child

God chose a young virgin of Nazareth to become the bearer of His greatest gift. She had to endure shame and embarrassment as her pregnancy became known. Think of the courage it took for Mary to tell her beloved Joseph that she was "with child." How she must have agonized over what was happening to her. Perhaps God knew the strength of this young girl from the very beginning. She must have relied on Him and the strength He gave her as she watched the events of Jesus' life unfold. Imagine the immense emotional pain and agony she felt as she watched her son being crucified. Mary survived a lifetime of confusion, grief, and joy over being the mother of the Son of God.

God Credits Women Teachers

In the New Testament, to whom does Paul give credit for teaching Timothy about the sacred writings? He praises Timothy's mother, Eunice, and his grandmother, Lois, for the sincere faith they passed on to Timothy, who became an ardent missionary for the Gospel.

God's Word is honest about life. It leaves out none of the gory details. But within the Word we also see the steadfastness of a loving heavenly Father as He chooses women of faith to carry out His plan. Your name may not be Rahab, Hannah, Mary, Lois, or Eunice, but the desires of our heavenly Father have not changed since biblical days. He still gives us opportunities to be part of His plan.

Resilience for the Journey

When you are on a trip or vacation, what do you do when the kids start hanging out the windows or the dog is crossing his legs? You take a rest stop! When you are driving a long distance and you have already played every CD with a lively beat and slapped your face several times to stay awake, what do you do? You take a rest stop. You stop the car, get out, walk around, breathe, go to the restroom, or get something to drink. Then you get back in, renewed with energy and open eyes, ready for the journey ahead. Following are some rest stop ideas to give you new strength, energy, and clearer vision. *Rest Stops for Resilience* will help you not only survive, but find your own unique way to thrive and become emotionally and spiritually healthy.

Crisis situations can easily cloud your vision. Practicing *Rest Stops for Resilience* will help you see straight when the tough times come.

Rest Stop 1: Breathe

This is not rocket science. Any kindergartner understands the significant relationship between breathing and living. But somehow as we grow up we forget this elementary truth. We inhale all sorts of other stuff, forgetting what really keeps us going. We move at such a fast pace, we do not take time to stop and smell anything but car fumes. One ordinary mother realized how her inability to slow down was affecting her children and vowed to make a difference in her lifestyle and theirs. She wanted something more. As a result of her courage and creativity, she impacted the lives of many. Here is Linda's story.

Linda was 36 years old and married to an architect who traveled frequently. She had three children, ages 10, 7, and 5. She volunteered to be the room mother in her daughter's kindergarten class, assisted in the school library three mornings a week, and taught an adult Bible study class at her church. With her art background, Linda was often called upon to help with special events at church and school. She also served on the mayor's committee to design art programs for the new children's museum in their town. When her husband was out of town, she was the only taxi driver, herding children from soccer to dance to piano lessons.

Linda knew that she felt tired all the time. She often battled infections, but just blamed it on allergies. Her fatigue began to take its toll and she too readily lost her patience and yelled at the kids. She felt tired when she woke up every morning and forced herself to get going on all the activities of the day. Gradually, she began forgetting details and was too tired after dinner to do anything with the family. She even noticed that her children were tired all the time too. Linda never felt like she had time to read the Bible, but picked it up one morning out of desperation and flipped to the book of Psalms. It was there her eyes and heart found two Scripture verses to cling to: "God is our refuge and strength, an ever-present help in trouble" (Psalm 46:1) and "Be still, and know that I am God; I will be exalted among the nations, I will be exalted in the earth" (Psalm 46:10).

Linda stopped. For the first time in what seemed like years, she just stopped. She stopped physically, emotionally, mentally, and spiritually, and breathed in the promise of Scripture. She knew that she was in trouble, and more than anything desired to know God. She called the school, the church, and the mayor's office and told them that she had something urgent to take care of for the next two weeks. To Linda, it *was* urgent. She desperately desired to change her lifestyle. For two weeks, she arose each morning, got the kids off to school, and sat down to read the Bible and pray. She took long walks and even longer bubble baths. She read a novel and organized her children's baby books. After two weeks, she was a new woman. It showed in her face, and her family noticed the difference. Linda could feel the difference. She thanked God for revealing Himself to her in quiet, still moments. Linda breathed in God's peace and love, motivating her to take stock of her life.

Linda knew she had to make a change, but she didn't want to completely drop out of things, so she suggested a compromise plan at school and church that allowed many other parents to be involved and not overworked. Linda suggested to the PTA that parents form teams and rotate responsibilities throughout the school year. No one parent would have the lead responsibility for more than half of the school year. Instead of one lead room parent, Linda suggested that parents sign up to be the organizer of one party or one field trip per year, spreading out the responsibility and work. The school gave the plan a probationary try for a year and loved it. Now, more parents are willing to volunteer because they can better handle the load. The team spirit is permeating every PTA-led activity.

Linda prayed about a solution to her church involvement. She approached the other teachers in her adult department and suggested that they take more of a team approach. They looked at the year and at their teaching gifts and expertise. Linda especially enjoyed teaching lessons from the Gospels on the life of Christ. Another teacher knew more about Old Testament history. The team divided up the Sundays and rotated the teaching responsibilities based on the lesson content. They enlisted individual class members to serve as ongoing care-group leaders who called and kept up with the group. It was more of a master teacher approach. The class members seem to be enjoying the rotation. It gives different perspectives to the Bible teaching and involves more members in caring for one another.

Linda found a college student who attended her church to help two afternoons a week when the children's activities caused scheduling conflicts. Their "student carpooler" has grown into more of an adopted big sister. The student baby-sits for Linda in exchange for free home-cooked meals and the use of Linda's laundry room.

Linda and her husband decided they were raising their children to be just as over-involved as their parents. Now, at the beginning of the school year, each child may choose only one activity in which to be involved. This has cut down on travel time and allowed for more free time at home. The children now climb trees and ride bikes instead of having to shuffle all over town for soccer practice, dance, music, all in the same day. Linda was and is a strong woman who loves the Lord and her family. Her lifestyle matched the trend of most families today. You might recognize it.

But Linda knew she wanted more out of her life than just feeling frustrated and fatigued every day. She desired a deeper relationship with her husband, children, and God, and she used the gifts God had given her to find a solution. Linda's vision for a new lifestyle will impact her children for the rest of their lives. Her influence has caused other families in her school and church to examine their priorities and find a new way of approaching life together.

We celebrate Linda's vision of courage and creativity. She stopped to breathe. Can you imagine if we all arranged our lives so that we could breathe in God's vision?

Rest Stop 2: Relax

Now that you have caught your breath and register a regular heart rhythm again, allow yourself some time to relax. We know: "Relax? What's that?" The wonderful point of relaxation is that it can mean different things to different people. The way we choose to relax might stress you out. We both remember times when we forgot the meaning of the word.

Ellen was the editor of two monthly magazines.

My workload was incredible, but I did not know how to lessen it. I kept more plates spinning than any Ed Sullivan act ever did! It seemed the better I performed, the more work I created for myself. I came home to family and church responsibilities. If you have teenagers, you know that there is seldom a dull moment.

I can remember a friend telling me to slow down

and relax some. I felt chaotic all the time. I would not allow myself to be inactive. Guilt would creep in if I wasn't working on a project of some kind. It finally dawned on me that I no longer knew how to relax. That's when I realized I was in trouble. I am not a big television watcher, but I made myself sit down and watch something with the kids. At first, I only wanted to watch programs with some educational value. Gradually, I let myself watch a show just to relax and laugh. I began to enjoy sitting down with my children and watching a program together.

Since that time, I have been very conscious of learning to relax. I started enjoying bubble baths, walks, music, and even reading for pleasure. My methods of relaxation come and go, but I make sure I do it. It is important to let my mind and my body do nothing but regroup. It is critical that I teach myself the art of relaxation.

Deb also knows the pain of over-involvement.

Several years ago at a women's Bible study I taught, I asked the members to pray for me to find strength in time management. "I can't prioritize my activities and feel like I'm headed for burnout," I shared openly.

For several days after the meeting I earnestly prayed for each woman's specific needs: for Karen's daughter who was ill; for Joan's husband to find work; for Susannah's marriage. I also waited patiently for my answer to prayer (well, as patient as I can be). Two weeks went by, and I honestly anticipated this profound miracle to help me get my life in order. Meanwhile, I continued to fill my days with the usual long list of commitments to others, leaving no time for myself.

Then ... He spoke. God answered my prayer and gave me ample time to evaluate my over-commitment with a rough case of the flu. I had the works—the high fever, chest cold, aches, and complaints. As I lay in bed moaning, my husband, Bob, had to find other people to handle the many activities I was in charge of: the Brownie cookie sales, swim team awards dinner, adult choir retreat, children's choir rehearsal, the women's Bible study group. I remember crying with a thermometer propped under my tongue and the fragrance of Vicks Vapor Rub surrounding my blankets as I shivered with fever; I certainly wasn't thinking of anything but getting well.

I spent a total of eight days in bed and only the top priority items got completed: our three children were fed, bathed, hugged, and put to bed. As I recovered, I remained weak for two more weeks and moped around the house in my robe. I began to appreciate the silence that went along with being alone. I started to read, daydream, and laugh more. Evenings were spent sitting with the family, talking and playing games instead of running to night meetings at the church and school. My friends began to call to let me know that activities and organizations were functioning smoothly. I realized I wasn't the only person who could lead the choir, teach the study group, and organize the community fundraiser.

During my timeout before burnout, I think the real moment of awakening came when my youngest daughter, Ashley, said with all honesty while lying beside me on the bed, "Mommy, I love you when you are sick. You have time to listen to me." Is your life cluttered with too many activities? As I experienced, over-zealous involvement in too many activities may cause suffering for your loved ones as well as for you, but God can help. Freedom from the stress and anxieties of a hurried life can happen when we move beyond "self" and turn humbly to our Lord for guidance. Only He can free us from the bondage of burnout and give us back the time of our life!

Be at rest once more, O my soul, for the Lord has been good to you. Psalm 116:7

We have found that after we let our brains relax, we begin to function with new creativity and strength. We also let others function as they choose. Sometimes when you are not allowing yourself to relax, you don't allow others the privilege of relaxation. Children often learn to be overactive from adults who can't sit still. As the 1998 *Calendar for Women Who Do Too Much* said, "What a relief! I just gave up the job of running the universe."

We say to you, "Give it up! Sit this one out awhile." Resilience demands focused energy. If you believe that it is okay to relax during the ordinary times of life, then when the chaotic times come, you will have formed a healthy habit. Relaxing becomes more vital during a crisis. Your body, mind, and spirit soar to solve a problem or deal with a difficult situation. If you do not step back and totally relax, your body cannot regroup and you will lose what little stamina is left. God invites us to breathe and relax in Him. He calls it rest.

> *"Come to Me all you who are weary and burdened, and I will give you rest. Take my yoke upon you and learn from Me, for I am gentle and humble in heart, and you will find rest for your souls. For My yoke is easy and My burden is light."* **Matthew 11:28–30**

Rest Stop 3: Look

It sounds like a simple request: look. Of course, we know it would help if we told you what to look for. There are several substantial things to look for, but how and where you look is just as important as what you look for. If your vision is not secure beforehand, you will lose sight of where you are headed when trouble and transition encamp around you. In order to stabilize your vision, you need first to breathe, then relax. When you are moving too quickly in a state of panic and chaos, your vision will be blocked by worry, fear, frustration, and confusion. When you are still and resting with God, you can see above the clouds of the storm. You can find God at work in the middle of your problems. Middle-aged mom, Janie, found God to be faithful in the midst of crisis.

Janie experienced an incredible year. An independent architect, she landed two big accounts that gave her just enough work to challenge her, but not to overwhelm her or take her away from her family time at home. Her girls were 12 and 10. Her husband, Justin, was traveling less, providing more family togetherness time. For several months, Janie prayed earnestly that God would take her deeper in her walk with Christ. She wanted to know Him more. She started attending a Bible study and prayer group. For the first time in her life, Janie felt the "peace that passes all understanding." She couldn't wait to read her Bible and spend time alone with God each day. Janie and Justin started a Bible study for couples in their home in an effort to reach out to more families in their community. Each week, the group grew and spiritual needs were met. At Christmas, the family went to Janie's parents' home for a delightful visit and then to the beach for a nice, relaxing time before returning home. Janie couldn't remember a more exciting time and looked forward to another incredible year. But in February, the unexpected happened. Janie's dad called to give extremely disturbing news. Her mom was in the hospital. She passed out after suffering from what she thought was another migraine. Her doctor ran tests and performed a subsequent biopsy, which revealed inoperable brain cancer. She was given three months to live. Janie, her dad, her sister, and a few church friends alternated staying at the hospital around the clock. After only three weeks, Janie's mom slipped into a coma. Instead of three months, Janie's mom died after six weeks. The whole family felt lost and in a state of shock.

Janie ached with grief. She could not imagine life without her mother. She held her girls and wept, knowing they would not know the future love and support of their grandmother. She hated the look in her dad's eyes. It was distant and untouchable. She couldn't help but cry out to God and ask *why*. Janie decided to stay with her dad for a few weeks to help him settle some matters. It was during this time that the God she rested with on a daily basis restored her sight.

In Janie's quest to find some answers, she turned to God daily. She told Him she wasn't sure how to pray, but believed He was with her and would not leave her. She begged God to make His presence real to her. She desperately needed to know He was still moving in her life.

The very first week after her mother's death, a young mother dropped by Janie's dad's house, bringing a casserole. She carried a baby and held the hand of a preschooler. When the girl spoke, it was evident she was not originally from the United States. She told Janie that Janie's mother was one of the first people to reach out to her family when they moved from Brazil. Her husband was in medical school at the nearby university. Janie's mom taught the girl English, stayed with her after the birth of her child, took her shopping, and introduced her to a new life in Christ.

In the middle of Janie's grief, she saw the hand of God. Instead of focusing on her loss, she clearly saw what she had gained through the influence and example of her mother. Janie looked for a word from God when she was hurting. He answered her prayer.

When crisis comes—and it will—ask the Lord for new eyes to see through the tears to find Him.

Look for things to thank Him for—a flower, a smile from a friend, or a baby sleeping through the night. Defeat your feelings of loneliness and depression with thankfulness. Even when you do not feel grateful, look harder for people and things to thank God for.

Look for Jesus at work: see Him move in a church service; listen to your child pray; hear a testimony of answered prayer. Even when life seems to fall apart around us, our Lord remains steadfast and His Holy Spirit continues to move in the lives of people.

I pray that out of His glorious riches He may strengthen you with power through His Spirit in your inner being, so that Christ may dwell in your hearts through faith. And I pray that you, being rooted and established in love, may have power, together with all the saints, to grasp how wide and long and high and deep is the love of Christ, and to know this love that surpasses knowledge—that you may be filled to the measure of all the fullness of God. Ephesians 3:16–19

Look for Jesus at work, changing you: wake up feeling more alive; see a familiar Scripture verse in a new, energizing way; experience a desire to reach out to others. After you have been through a difficult time, as the Lord begins healing your spirit, He will accomplish His work with grace and love. He meets you where you are.

The way someone else handles a crisis and recovers is not necessarily the way you will. God created you and understands your unique needs. He deals with each of us individually. His love is patient and kind. He desires for you to be whole again. He will not leave you or forsake you. If you fear that your life will never be the same again, you are exactly right. After troubling times, life changes and we change, but God never does. He will create a new work in you and begin again using you to make a difference.

> *I thank my God every time I remember you. In all my prayers for all of you, I always pray with joy because of your partnership in the gospel from the first day until now, being confident of this, that He who began a good work in you will carry it on to completion until the day of Christ Jesus.* Philippians 1:3–6

> *Then you will call upon Me and come and pray to Me, and I will listen to you. You will seek Me and find Me when you seek Me with all your heart.* Jeremiah 29:12

It is time to pull over the car, get out, and take a break. Spiritual strength is a paradox. To build your strength up, you must stop, breathe, relax, and look. Pump up by slowing down and rediscovering God's love.

CHAPTER 6

Women with Vision Build Bridges:

Connect Socially

"We just can't talk." That's how Ginny describes her relationship with Sam, her husband of 23 years. When the two sit down at night to talk about their young adult children, church events, or even their favorite television shows, the conversation is strained and awkward. Ginny tells of not knowing what to say to Sam, feeling intimidated by his statements, and almost wishing the moment was over.

"I get so nervous when we try to communicate with anyone, even my neighbors. Sometimes my heart beats faster, and I can't think of the right words to say. I guess I've always hidden behind the kids. Until this time in my life, I've never had to talk to someone with no diversions. Now that the kids are gone, I have no choice."

If you are like millions of women and have spent much of your life hiding behind kids, commitments, or career, it's time to step out and become socially connected and focus on your communication skills. Communication is necessary for women who seek to build bridges in relationships as they follow God's vision. When communication breaks down, the marriage and family break down; work relationships suffer; and close friends become distant. In fact, when communication breaks down, everything breaks down! Remember the spaceship Columbia? Many of us will never forget the moment. After years of preparation, frustration, and tremendous cost over-runs, the spaceship Columbia sat poised on launch pad 39 ready for lift-off. Millions watched around the world. Then, suddenly and unexpectedly, the countdown was halted. Everything stood still. Finally, we watched in disappointment as the astronauts climbed back down out of the cabin, and the entire launch was delayed for two days. Why? Because two computers couldn't talk to each other!

Who hasn't dealt with computer problems on the job or at home? Well, real-life communication is even more complex and so very important to relationships. Communication is so important that one magazine poll of more than 30,000 women revealed that only one problem ranked above conflicts over money in the family—and that was poor communication.

Building Intimate Bridges

The purpose of communication is to understand one another's expectations, needs, feelings, and interests.

Developing effective communication skills can enhance great relationships and help stabilize rocky ones. Nonetheless, we all experience life's interruptions, including loss of employment, death of a parent or best friend, loss of a child, or illness in a spouse, that test our ability to communicate with love. Without connecting socially or having open communication, these life interruptions will almost certainly leave you with the inevitable: lack of intimacy in relationships, an unhappy marriage, broken family ties, or division between friends.

Real communication—building intimate bridges with those around you—involves:

- Saying what you feel
- Saying it clearly
- Listening to what the other person says
- Making sure you are hearing accurately

Although communication gaps—even with other Christians—are a fact of life, there are ways to bridge the gaps as you strive to become genuine and approachable in your relationships.

How Well Do You Communicate?

Just as some women are called to teach and others are called to nurture, some of us have the gift of being able to communicate well with others. Our friend Candy has such a gift. As the director of a church preschool, she seems to attract people like a pied piper. When you see Candy at the church preschool, it is with a circle of friends surrounding her. She is intent on answering questions, listening to problems, and addressing concerns. To watch her as she connects socially with others, you can tell that her attention is focused directly on the person speaking. No matter how many preschoolers are tugging at her dress, trying to get attention, Candy stands attentive to the person speaking. She leans her body forward as if to say, "I really care about what you are saying," and looks the person directly in the eyes—never allowing herself to be distracted by others. She has been gifted with excellent communication skills.

What does it take to learn to communicate effectively with your husband, your children, your friends, and neighbors? After talking with numerous Christian women across the nation, we identified the following 10 key precepts that are necessary to bridge communication gaps in your life. After reading through the list, check those that you might work on.

Ten Bridge-Building Precepts

A woman who is socially connected is:

1. **Approachable.** You can talk to those around you without hesitation or fear; others are not intimidated.

2. **Able to show genuine concern.** You are never too preoccupied but can give others undivided attention during communication.

3. **Open-minded.** You can express yourself with others and speak in a manner they can understand.

4. **Not quick to place blame.** You recognize that discomfort is a part of living, and that you need to assume responsibility for your own life at some point. You have learned to cope with difficulties in daily living.

5. **Able to exhibit concern by your mannerism and tone of voice.** You are aware that words have the power to lift someone up or tear him down, depending on how they are used. Instead of communicating in anger and harshness, you speak in a non-threatening manner.

6. **Responsible.** You respect those around you and speak in a reverent manner.

7. **A Fair "Fighter."** When there are arguments (and most relationships have some or someone is getting stomped on!), you do not throw dirt—insults, past history, name-calling and unnecessary fuel for the flames.

8. **Considered "safe."** Experiencing emotional safety in communication is necessary to establish intimacy, openness, and passion with those around you.

9. **Not one to hold a grudge.** You know that clinging to a grudge is counterproductive and keeps you from dealing with the problem that initially led you to the grudge. You understand that resentment breeds discontent.

10. **One who forgives and forgets.** Not only can you forgive the other for a wrongdoing as Jesus taught, but you also can forget the incident and move on in a positive manner.

Focus on Others with Bridge-Builders

As much as we would like, not many of us can have these qualities every day. Yet we have personally experienced that no matter how deficient we are in our communication skills, in order to seek and follow God's vision in our lives, we can and must master these precepts. In doing so, we can erase relationship stumbling blocks from the past and move on to greater understanding and love.

How can you begin? Check out the following bridge-builders you can use.

Bridge-Builder 1: Learn to Listen

In the book *Bus 9 to Paradise*, Leo Buscaglia tells about boarding a flight to New York. The flight attendant shouted with delight when he entered the plane. "I've wanted to meet you for such a long time. May I talk with you later?" she asked. When she got a break, the young woman sat next to him and frantically told her story—a cheating husband, a disturbed child, a feeling of despondency and helplessness, a fear of being unable to cope. After a long while, she stopped mid-sentence and sighed deeply with relief. She wiped her tears and sat up in the seat. "Oh, Dr. Buscaglia," she said, "you've helped me so much."[2] Dr. Buscaglia had not even uttered a word. What a tremendous ministry it is just to listen.

Being an effective listener is vital in establishing a caring rapport with others. When feelings and thoughts are poured out and real listening occurs, the speaker feels loved and understood. Listening doesn't mean getting ready to jump on the other person with your half of the argument. It means tuning in to what is being said and really hearing the message.

It is amazing how well we listen to a good friend when we are interested in the subject. But what happens when we are not interested? Often we tune out the conversation, ignore the person speaking, and use all sorts of body language to let the other know we are not interested in her thoughts or opinions.

Self-Assessment

How do you rate as a listener? Check the following to assess your listening skills.

- Do you listen to the needs of family members and friends and really hear what is being said?
- Do you weigh each situation with compassion and empathy?
- Do you see everything in life as totally black or white with no room for compromise?

As Christian women of vision, we can look to the perfect example of Jesus Christ for excellence in communication skills. Jesus patiently listened to each person who approached Him, empathized with their problems, and shared selfless love with others.

Bridge-Builder 2: Learn to Interpret Body Language

Communication doesn't mean just talking or listening; it includes all the clues to a person's feelings—his bearing, expression, resignation. Everyone around you uses signs, symbols, body language, smiles, and other gestures to express caring and love. People don't always have to say, "I'm hurting," or "I'm in need." A quick glance tells you that. Women of vision who are good communicators can detect problems with others by observing nonverbal clues such as:

- slammed doors
- unusual silence at mealtime
- spending time alone in the bedroom
- locked doors for long periods of time
- behavior that regresses—temper fits, crying jags, hitting siblings
- sullen looks
- restlessness
- insomnia
- lack of appetite or overeating
- irritability

As you work toward greater communication at home, on the job, and in the community, try to let others know they are accepted—unconditionally. Taking time to sit with the person, really listening, and trying to understand where he or she is coming from are all vital principles of being a good communicator. Others will feel free to express their innermost thoughts to you; a relationship will be formed.

Bridge-Builder 3: Show Empathy

In the gospels, Jesus teaches us a lifestyle that is full of empathy, of being sensitive to those around us. This selfless love Jesus shares enables us to meet the personal needs of those around us, rather than tearing them down. Compassion, sincerity, and empathy communicate your feelings of friendship and support. As you work to think before you speak, consider the following:

- How would I like to hear the message?

- How would it feel to hear these words?
- Would it enable me to grow as a person?
- How could the words be stated so growth can occur in our relationship?

Messages given in a caring setting are more likely to be taken and acted upon. Positive truths spoken in love enhance your friendship. But if you share negative opinions critically and thoughtlessly, you will only destroy the communication at hand.

Bridge-Builder 4: Watch Your Body Language

Often, body language speaks louder than words, especially when we are upset. Body language can make the difference between honest comments being accepted graciously or being rejected in despair.

As you seek God's vision for your life, you may be dealing with new relationships—at church, at work, in the community. Just as people use body language to express their feelings of caring and love, they also use it to show distrust, disgust, and anger. While body language usually occurs subconsciously, it makes up 90 percent of effective communication. The way you sit or stand, the way you cross your legs, and the way you gesture or smile while you listen greatly affects how the other person feels.

Facial expressions also can enhance or detract from your listening skills. An affable, responsive face can be a tremendous asset when communicating with others. Your expressions can share confidence and conviction as someone confides in you with openness. And if you make eye contact and keep it, your eyes will pick up how the person is responding to what you say. As you begin to connect socially and build communication bridges, try these techniques:

- Avoid insults, but be very specific about what the problem is.
- Avoid using hopeless talk, such as "this always happens ..."
- State the actual problem; don't throw blame.
- Don't label others "lazy," "sloppy," or "selfish."
- Don't use absolutes such as "you always ..." or "you never ..."

Bridge-Builder 5: Encourage Others to Express True Feelings

If you've worked at home for a period of time and are now moving out into the world as you pursue God's vision, it's important to be an enabler. This means that you are the safe catalyst who enables those around you to express their innermost feelings without fear of betrayal.

During times of intimate conversation with others, try the following:

- Interject some personal history.
- Tell of spiritual struggles you've had.
- Share how God helped you cope with crises or disappointments.
- Talk about the feelings you experienced—fear, nervousness, emptiness.

As you risk being open, and talk about your life struggles as a Christian, others will feel a sense of trust and be able to express their feelings within the safety net of this relationship.

Bridge-Builder 6:
Communicate Compassion

Compassion is the ability to feel with another person. When others express their innermost feelings, ask yourself, "Do I have any understanding of the experiences that have brought him or her to this place in life?" "Is there anything I can do to make his life or her life easier and more meaningful?"

Having compassion is a wonderful asset for women of vision. There is a story about two brothers who were spending their last days together in a nursing home. The brother in the bed closest to the window was warm, talkative, outgoing, optimistic, and altogether very sociable. The brother next to the door was blind, negative, and quite lonely.

One day the brother next to the door asked the brother next to the window to describe for him the things that were going on outside. The brother next to the window took great delight in doing so. He described colorful flowers bursting into bloom and delicate hummingbirds feeding from the buds; he told how mothers were pushing babies in strollers and children were laughing on the playground. This became a daily ritual as the jovial brother next to the window described to his blind brother the flurry of activity outside. The brother who was blind lived for these reports from outside. But one day, the sensitive, extroverted brother next to the window died, and his bed was taken by another man. "Would you please describe for me," asked the sur-viving brother next to the door, "what is going on outside our window?" The new roommate looked out the window in puzzlement and then looked back at the man, and said, "I don't see what good it would do, my friend. There is noth-ing outside this window except a dirty brick wall."

This story illustrates how God calls us all to come together and "feel with" one another. God gives us compas-sion. Think about your relationships—at home, at work, at church, or in the community. Does someone have a stum-bling block you can help with? Is there a member who is experiencing conflict, and you can offer empathy? Do you know someone who is bitter from past failures? Can you help him see God's plan for his life?

In Paul's letter to the Ephesians, he writes, "It was He who gave some to be apostles, some to be prophets, some to be evangelists, and some to be pastors and teachers, to pre-pare God's people for works of service, so that the body of Christ may be built up until we all reach unity in the faith and in the knowledge of the Son of God and become mature, attaining to the whole measure of the fullness of Christ" (Ephesians 4:11–13).

The amazing affirmation that Paul makes here is that all of these differences are given to us to help us build one another up to maturity and to grow in love. It is when we push and tug against one another in caring relationships that we begin to discover who we are; we begin to grow into the women God intended us to be. It is when we compas-sionately reach out to others "even though ..." that God will bless our lives.

Healthy communication involves a kind of transformation—the movement from that place where we wish everyone was like us to the place where we become so accustomed to their idiosyncrasies and their special quirks that we wonder how we ever got along without them. Although that sounds difficult, under the direction of our loving God, all the unique parts of His body—the Church—work together so the body can build itself up and grow in love.

Bridge-Builder 7: Speak the Truth in Love

Also in Ephesians, Paul urges us to "speak the truth in love" (Ephesians 4:15). This means that in all our relationships we work to speak plainly and clearly with one another. Sometimes we have to say, "I am angry" or "I am hurt" or "I am disappointed." When we can trust our own feelings and face the truth of who we are, then we can move forward as a unit.

There is danger at the other end of the spectrum. Just as there are those who cannot speak the truth to those they love, there are others who use the truth as a club to beat others into submission and to blackmail others to get their own way. Paul does not tell us to simply "speak the truth." He admonishes that we are to "speak the truth in love" saying, "Do not let any unwholesome talk come out of your mouths, but only what is helpful for building others up according to their needs, that it may benefit those who listen. And do not grieve the Holy Spirit of God, with whom you were sealed for the day of redemption. Get rid of all bitterness, rage and anger, brawling and slander, along with every form of malice. Be kind and compassionate to one another, forgiving each other, just as in Christ God forgave you" (Ephesians 4:29–32).

Bridge-Builder 8: Communicate Caring through Touch

The significance of touch in human development was first identified in the 1940s. Many institutionalized infants, who were either homeless or had been orphaned because of the war, suffered from what doctors then called marasmus—which literally means wasting away—now known as failure to thrive. Fed but unloved, some babies even died. Those who survived showed impaired physical and mental development.

However, doctors discovered that just a few minutes a day of talking, maintaining eye contact, and stroking helped these hospitalized babies grow and mature at the same rate as home-reared babies. The reason these babies could not thrive seemed to lie in a lack of contact that gave the message, "No one is here to care for you."

Touch is critical in becoming genuine with those around you. A pat on the shoulder, a hug, or a firm handshake often generates a stronger sense of caring and concern than spoken words.

Deb remembers visiting Grandma Bruce, a resident in the Alzheimer's unit at a South Florida nursing home, one last time.

Since our older children had been away at college, they had not seen their 91-year-old great-

grandmother for several years. The last memory they had of her was hurrying around her small home while fixing breakfast on a weekend trip. But this visit was different. As we were escorted into the guarded Alzheimer's unit and observed the men and women staring blankly into space, I could tell our children were becoming increasingly nervous.

"What do I say to her?" Ashley asked anxiously as she grabbed my hand. "How will she know who we are?"

The nurse forewarned us that Grandma usually forgets where her room is, and after a lengthy search, we finally found my grandmother peacefully asleep in someone else's bed. Far from the smiling, active woman our children remembered, Grandma was now tiny, delicate, and fragile.

"Grandma?" I rubbed her back gently. "Grandma, it's Deb."

Grandma slowly sat up in the bed, and stared blankly at our family. Looking at her confused expression, I knew that she didn't know who we were. And while her trembling mouth made it difficult for her to speak, she touched my hand and smiled broadly, saying, "I like that."

With memories of years past flashing through my mind, I continued to lovingly rub Grandma's back. Brittnye and Ashley then took Grandma's cold, wrinkled hands and began to massage them gen-

tly, as if they were breathing their youth into the elderly woman's body. Bob found a soft blanket to wrap around her, and Rob helped to lift Grandma into her wheelchair. Soon the entire family was touching her in some way, while she kept smiling, saying, "Oh, I like that. Yes, I like that."

Grandma didn't know who we were, but she knew that someone special loved her. She affirmed the one form of communication everyone understands—the miracle of touch. This nonverbal form of love can be used with young and old alike as you interact in an affirming way—no words, just gentle hugs, pats, and caresses.

In His ministry, Jesus expressed concern and healed many persons through the use of His hands. In the story of Jesus' receiving the little children despite His disciples' objections, "He took the children in His arms, put His hands on them and blessed them" (Mark 10:16). When Peter's mother-in-law was ill, Jesus "touched her hand and the fever left her" (Matthew 8:15).

Can't you visualize our Lord lifting His arms around children, lifting up the lame, and embracing those in pain? As He preached loving concern, He also demonstrated it. He reached out with gentle, caring hands, touching cold and empty lives with His power.

How many times each day do our husbands and children need that gentle stroke, supportive hug, or warm caress? Anger or hostility can sometimes be alleviated with a person's warm, forgiving embrace.

In the midst of your busy workweek, remind yourself that a caring touch is often the comfort and security your loved ones long for. Even though you may feel nervous stepping out to pursue God's direction, those around you share the same feelings. Coworkers, classmates, community volunteers, or church members may be hiding behind masks or feeling insecure about their place in life. By giving a loving touch, you may be adding to the security they need.

Bridge-Builder 9: Learn Creative Conflict Resolution

For many women of vision, conflict is one part of relationships—whether at home, at work, or volunteering—that is not pleasant. Even the most vibrant and caring Christians experience conflict from time to time. Whatever the source of conflict, creative problem solving is an excellent way of opening doors of compromise. Use the following steps:

1. State the problem at hand.

2. List all alternatives. Have fun with this and brainstorm creatively.

3. What are the pros (or benefits) and cons of each alternative? What is the worst outcome? What is the best outcome?

4. Select the choice that meets the most positive needs with the least consequences.

5. Make a decision and try it.

Creative Conflict Resolution

Problem	Alternatives	Pros/Cons
1.	1.	1.
2.	2.	2.
3.	3.	3.

In avoiding conflict that leads to disaster, it is vital that women of vision model positive ways of handling differences. Others will look to you for keys in dealing with opposition.

Bridge-Builder 10: Overcome Personal Barriers to Open Communication

Women of vision are challenged to seek God's will for their lives. Sometimes, this involves taking risks outside the realm of "security." For Linda, a teacher's aide at an elementary school, taking risks meant overcoming a lifetime of shyness and standing up to her principal about unfair gossip among the teachers.

"I put my job on the line," Linda said. "But some of the teachers were spreading horrible rumors about the teacher's aides, and it was mean-spirited." Going in to her appointment with the principal, Linda felt anxious and hardly knew what to say. Yet after opening up about the problem, Linda said she felt an inner strength from God and she knew what she had done was right.

Judith, a gifted watercolor artist, had never shown any of her paintings for fear of criticism. For years, she was known in her neighborhood as the quiet woman who never came out of the house. Little did friends and neighbors know that Judith spent hours each day working on detailed paintings. "I never told anyone I could draw or paint," Judith said, "because I was afraid they would critique my work. Then last year I saw an advertisement in the paper calling for amateur artists to display their work in an outdoor art fair. The proceeds from the fair were to go to a local shelter for women and children. Something inside me—perhaps the voice of God—nudged me to volunteer my talent."

Deb tells of not submitting her first article to a youth leaders' magazine until her mother repeatedly fussed at her that she should use her talent. "I was afraid! I was afraid of talking with the editor of the magazine to discuss my idea. I just knew they would not like what I had to say. I was afraid of being rejected. Then not only did I sell the first submission, but I sold almost every one I wrote for that magazine."

What barriers do you face in communicating openly? Try the following solutions.

Word block: I cannot think of what to say.

Solution: Breathe deeply, and say nothing. Smile until the words come to you.

Super shy: I'm going to pass out if I have to speak in front of anyone.

Solution: They are just people! Imagine they are your best friends and even give them imaginary names to help you relax.

Tongue-tied: The wrong words come out of my mouth.

Solution: Slow down. Don't try to answer questions so quickly. Take a breath, then slowly respond.

Too talkative: I talk too much! It's because I'm nervous.

Solution: Nervousness can make you say more than you normally would. Try intentionally *not* to talk. Breathe deeply, then think before you utter words.

As a woman of vision, you are called to build bridges as you connect socially with family, friends, and a host of people in your life. It's not always easy to break out of your comfort zones and speak up for yourself or others. Nonetheless, as you continue to read this book, you will gain the much-needed confidence to believe in yourself and trust that the Lord is with you in every connection you make.

CHAPTER 7

Women with Vision Are Passionate about Life:

Connect Intimately

When Deb called one of her neighbors recently, the answering machine responded with the following message, "Hi, this is Julie. I am home for the evening but can't come to the phone. In fact, unless it's an emergency, I don't want to talk. Okay! You can call me a homebody ... but just don't call me!"

Cocooning is an epidemic today. Because of juggling kids and careers, many women are exhausted, stressed, and anxious, and relish weekends as a time to lock the door to the outside world. Perhaps you can relate to having too much to do and not enough time to do it. For most women, harried days are filled with obstacles, diversions, and expectations. Has our society turned into such a rat race that the only way we can cope is to close the door and hide? Maybe.

Protection from Intimacy

Cocooning gives isolation or protection, but not all women enjoy being isolated. Your preference partially depends on if you are an introvert or extrovert. Introverts and extroverts have different ways of regrouping and relaxing to recharge their batteries after doing battle in today's world. Which are you?

Extrovert

You recharge your batteries by going to a party or sports event. Extroverts tend not to cocoon because the desire to be alone or withdraw isn't in their nature.

Introvert

You recharge your batteries by giving yourself space or simply by being alone. You thrive on cocooning because it helps you relax and regroup.

So perhaps some women cocoon because of their introverted nature. Or perhaps it is because they are on the brink of burnout, cocooning to seek refuge from stressed lives. For most of us, stress is an everyday word, with job and financial problems as the leading stressors. For those who work outside the home, even when we leave the office for the day, any downtime is spent negotiating deals with clients on cellular phones or answering faxes and e-mail at home. Whether you are dealing with downsizing, mergers, and layoffs, or kids, carpools, and housework, it is no news that many of us work 24 hours a day, seven days a week—even when we are not officially "at work."

Every week, some 95 million Americans suffer a stress-related problem and take medication for their aches and pains.[3] Whether it stems from phones ringing off the hook, being bombarded with news of crime and violence around the world, or living with rebellious teens who won't stop testing the limits—stress inundates the body with stress hormones that don't quit, creating a host of unpleasant physical symptoms. How have we learned to de-stress? It's simple. We turn off the phone and lock the door; we cocoon during our downtime.

We Have Lost Our Social Network

But there is a much greater problem that occurs when we clam up and keep to ourselves. According to sociologists, cocooning is a widespread symptom of a transient society where people have lost their social network. In years past, people lived close to family members and relied on parents and siblings for affirmation and emotional strength, even after marriage. When suffering occurred, people could turn to relatives for comfort and support. But with our highly mobile society, most adults today live hundreds of miles away from parents and siblings. We are not used to having our doorbell ring at all hours of the day or having extended family members living next door or even in our homes.

But this social support that our ancestors experienced is important. Close relationships and intimate connections with family and friends allow us to nourish our hungry souls. When we are tied emotionally to those we love, we can let out our feelings of fear, insecurity, and guilt, and receive comfort from people who accept us—just as we are—with no strings attached. But if we have no place that feels safe enough to let down our emotional defenses, we tend to keep our guard up all the time—a dissatisfied and troubled guard that numbly masks the very afflictions we are facing.

While cocooning may help us feel less stressful as we withdraw after a busy week, it certainly does not offer protection against stress. Research on stress-resistant personality traits has identified keys to staying healthy. They include:

- Involvement in work or other tasks that have great meaning
- The ability to relate well to others
- The ability to interact in a strong social network

More and more studies in the field of phychoneuroimmunology (PNI or mind/body interplay) are finding that the people most vulnerable to illness are those who are socially isolated.

"Wait a minute!" you might say. "I thought I was de-stressing by shutting out society and all its problems." If you really want to de-stress, unlock your door and invite company over for dinner.

In study after study, the findings were the same. That is, people with many social contacts—a spouse, a close-knit family, a network of friends, church, or other group affiliations—lived longer and had better health. In fact, those who had few ties with other people died at rates two to five times higher than those with good social ties.[4]

If used appropriately, taking time out is important in our hurried, fast-paced lives as we rekindle love, positive thinking, and physical energy. Jesus told the apostles, "Come with Me by yourselves to a quiet place and get some rest" (Mark 6:31). This is an important reminder for us that rest is a safety valve from pressure.

Jesus set a good example for us when He retreated to be alone with God. When He prayed and meditated on the hillside, Jesus put aside daily concerns and asked God for new power for living. This time out renewed His spirit and enabled Him to live out His ministry.

But don't forget that after Jesus was rested, He went out again among the masses, healing, preaching, and teaching the Word of God.

The problem arises when we spend too much time alone as we cocoon. This can be a symptom of a greater problem—social isolation. On the one hand, you may be purposely avoiding some people or the problems you have to face each day. In that case, you find your home a secure haven where you are not on display and where there are loved ones around to meet your needs. On the other hand, you may be facing symptoms of mild depression. These symptoms include loss of the desire to be with friends or engage in social activities.

Depression generally occurs when negative thoughts compound themselves and get so rooted in the subconscious that the person cannot break out of the cycle of negativism and self-pity. If left untreated, depression can last for months or even years. It can lead to feelings of helplessness and, at worst, suicide. It is not a sign of personal weakness or moral corruption. People can no more pull themselves together and get over depression than they can will away diabetes.

Depression comes in several forms, from a major depressive episode to a chronic, low-grade depression called dysthymia. Dysthymia is defined as being in a depressed mood more days than not for at least two years.

Symptoms of depression can include:
- disturbances in sleep patterns
- loss of interest in usual activities
- weight loss or gain (more than 5 percent of body weight)
- fatigue
- impaired thinking
- thoughts of dying or suicide
- depressed thoughts or irritability
- mood swings
- staying at home all the time
- avoidance of special friends
- difficulty concentrating
- feelings of worthlessness or excessive or inappropriate guilt
- agitation or, in contrast, a general slowing of intentional bodily activity

As many as 12 to 14 million Americans are affected with depression each year. This figure extends to as many as 13 to 20 percent of the total population in the United States having depression at any given time. And most researchers find that twice as many women suffer depression as men.

Depression is a very complicated affliction, but if you have the symptoms listed above on a regular basis, you should seek professional help and receive a proper diagnosis. Follow your physician's advice in taking medication and/or receiving therapy to alleviate the problem. Also consider the following.

- See a qualified mental health specialist if depression is immobilizing you. There are reports that up to 85 percent of patients will find relief through treatment with antidepressant medications, psychotherapy, or electroshock therapy.

- If you have suicidal thoughts, take them seriously and seek professional help.

- Alcohol and drugs cannot combat depression. Make certain that you only use medication prescribed by your physician.

- Just as in relieving stress, exercise is a great cure for easing mild depression. Determine what you can do physically and ask your doctor about an exercise program.

- It is important for depressed individuals to stick to a routine each day. Staying in bed "cocooning" all day because you have malaise will not help you alleviate the depressed feelings.

- Reaching out to help others is a great way to get out of depression. It greatly reduces actions such as brooding, moping, or too much introspection.

Taking Action

If cocooning has become a barrier between you and the outside world, there are workable steps you can take to break out of this behavior.

1. Recognize when you've set up hurdles in your relationships. If you have worked hard all week and make

a decision to be alone with your family on Friday night, that is healthy. But when you stay home day and night, week after week, and pull out of social activities, you need to evaluate your behavior. Are you hiding from relationships? Are you overextended and have no energy to enjoy friends and family? Are you suffering from mild depression?

2. Get your priorities in order so you have time and energy for socialization. Freedom from the stress and anxieties of a hurried life can only happen when you move beyond "self" and turn humbly to the Lord for guidance. Only He can free you from the bondage of an over-committed and meaningless life.

3. As you cut back your commitments, start to focus on moving beyond yourself and connecting intimately into the lives of others. Starting with one day a week, make plans to be with other people. This could include inviting friends over for a cookout on Saturday afternoon, or going out to lunch after church on Sunday. Most of us get into the pattern of "doing nothing" and forget how invigorating it is to be around other people.

4. Realize that as you break your habit of cocooning and begin to socialize with others, you are helping your health and well-being. Think of socialization as not only good for the mind and spirit, but as immunization against disease.

Be Selective

Being selective involves deciding when cocooning is appropriate and when it becomes obsessive; only you can make that decision. The biggest detriment for Christian women who cocoon and shut themselves out from intimate friendships is that they also cut themselves off from the blessings of these relationships. At that point, cocooning is a spiritual issue.

When you isolate yourself from other Christians, you are accepting less than what God has planned for you. In this regard, cocooning can create a barrier around you and your home which blocks others from entering your life.

There is no denying that we are a hurried generation. Most of us have very little time to sit down with our family for a meal, visit with in-laws and friends, hug our children, listen to our spouses, know our neighbors, or even pray. In this regard, cocooning or taking time out for rekindling a harried spirit can be a gentle reprieve from the hurriedness of our society.

However, if find yourself "addicted" to cocooning and the only social activity you get is flipping channels or surfing the Internet, perhaps you need to re-evaluate your commitments and make some plans to get involved in the lives of others. Putting feet to faith is an excellent place to start!

Put Feet to Faith

Our friend Judith sat at the table in Deb's kitchen while we were researching for a seminar. We thought she had lost her best friend.

"Pete's 40th birthday was yesterday," she said as she stirred her coffee. "I had thought about having a big surprise party with all of his close friends. I even called a caterer to price the meal and bought the cutest invitations. But the twins are so demanding now, and Kim is going through her adolescent pitfalls. I'm so overwhelmed with the kids that I never went through with the plans."

We both empathized—we have been full of wonderful intentions to care for others, such as the day Ellen was to volunteer at the school carnival, but forgot to write it on her calendar. Or the day Deb promised to take her young nephew to the zoo but didn't remember until he called later that evening. Both times we became so wrapped up in life's little interruptions that loving actions did not take place. While good intentions to help others are admirable, unless action takes place, they have no meaning. Women of vision make a living by what we get out of life, but we make a life by what we give. We are given a challenge to begin a lifestyle of good intentions and deeds in 1 John 3:18: "Little children, let us stop just *saying* we love people; let us *really* love them, and *show it* by our *actions*" (TLB).

It is difficult to follow through with kind deeds when your day is crammed with wiping noses, changing diapers, carpooling to school events, or working full-time away from home—then having to do "home work" at night. But if you organize for caring, it only takes a few minutes each day to connect physically with those around you, sharing your passion for life and love. Let the following steps help you put feet to faith.

Step 1: Organize for Action

Using a method as simple as a 5 × 7-inch card file box can help. On separate cards, write information of friends and family, such as name, address, phone number, birth date, anniversary date, sizes, favorite colors or collections, and so on. This information, along with a calendar, is the key to organized caring that can fit in any busy woman's schedule.

Check your calendar each week. What marked dates are coming up? Pull the cards of family members celebrating birthdays or anniversaries that week. Also pull cards of friends, neighbors, or teachers. If someone is having a special honor such as a graduation or award presentation in the next few weeks, pull this card too.

These cards represent people that you must focus on that week either by a prayer, personal visit, mail, phone, or planning a special celebration.

If you're computer savvy, you can set this system up on your home computer. Use a contacts list or address book feature to keep the vital information and then set your electronic calendar to notify you on the appropriate dates.

Step 2: Keep a "To Do" List Handy

Using the cards you have pulled, write down all your good intentions to touch the lives of these special people, and keep this memo nearby.

On Deb's refrigerator, she has an ongoing list with such notes as:

- Call Susan after her surgery Tuesday.
- Plan Ashley's party.
- Help Mrs. Peters grade papers Thursday.
- Send Grandma balloons for her 90th birthday.
- Spend time with Britta.

• Get gift for Mom and Dad's anniversary.

As she completes each intention, she checkmarks the reminder and adds to her list. She then takes the cards taped to her refrigerator, and puts them back into the file box. This one list is her constant cue to care for those who are important in her life.

Step 3: Set Aside a "Caring Time"

The time after lunch is when Deb phones friends, plans personal and family activities, writes letters or cards, or makes notes as she thinks of special needs. Ellen has a "caring time" late in the afternoon, after all her meetings are completed. Another busy mom we know blocks one morning a week to send cards, call friends, or volunteer at her son's school. What's most important is to find the "caring time" that is right for you, and make it a priority. The only way you can connect physically with others—putting feet to faith—is to set aside time and not let other interruptions intervene.

Step 4: Act on Impulse with Random Acts of Kindness

The Bible teaches us that "faith without works is dead" (James 2:20 KJV). When you feel a nudge to call a lonely friend, visit a neighbor, or stop your work to hug your child, do it now! The longer you wait between the mere thought and the actual deed, the less likely you are to follow through.

A philosophy professor we know challenges his students to be spontaneous in sharing feelings. "Say those special words 'I love you' aloud," he tells them. "Call a friend with your voice, visit that shut-in with your body, and hug your spouse or child with warm, caring arms. Take action, for only as you personally involve yourself in caring for others will your life be complete. It is through giving to others that you are rooted in the world."

Women of vision are called to be "rooted in Christ," which gives rich meaning to our lives. Our professor friend has a point about the power of actions; when we are rooted in Christ, we respond to those around us out of love and really touch lives. Random acts of kindness are contagious! Use these ideas to connect intimately with those around you.

- Call someone who is lonely.
- Call your parents and your siblings.
- Make dinner for a friend who is ill.
- Go to the movie with a family member.
- Take flowers to your neighbor.
- Write a letter to a long-lost friend or teacher from school.
- Renew an old friendship.
- Offer to watch someone's children or pet.
- Tell someone you are thinking about him or her.
- Plant flowers in your yard for others to see.
- Have a heart-to-heart talk with a coworker.
- Let someone get in front of you in the grocery store checkout line.
- Invite a friend to exercise with you.
- Make an un-birthday cake for a friend and celebrate.

- Go on a walk and smile at a stranger.
- Laugh aloud with a friend.

Step 5: Take Advantage of Modern Communication

If you can't visit someone to let her know you care, a phone call is a good way to show your concern for her. Keep the conversation focused on her, and be encouraging and personal. Spend time listening while on the telephone; you may pick up clues about the other person that could alert you to future dates, events, or even problems she is having in her life. Ellen's family has a standing phone date on Saturday at 4:00 P.M. when phone calls are exchanged with grandparents. Deb talks with her family members through e-mail and finds that they stay in touch daily using the Internet.

Send cards and letters to let others know you care. It's a good idea to keep a box of birthday, anniversary, and thank-you cards on hand, as well as stamps. Then you don't have any excuses!

Step 6: Pray

Prayer and actions go hand in hand. Pray for family and friends during your "caring time." Often, because of family budgets, you just can't call that friend long distance. But prayer can be a special communication tool you can use to let God know of your feelings and concern. After you pray for loved ones, let them know they are in your thoughts with a personal note.

Deb tells of a time she felt a powerful nudge from the

Holy Spirit to put feet to faith.

I don't know what made me sit down that rainy Tuesday morning and write that letter to Allene, my friend of 20 years. But a persistent voice inside me kept saying her name over and over. As I finally responded and put pen to paper, I wondered why I would think of her suddenly when we hadn't seen each other in more than 15 years. Allene Eley and her family were active members of Belvedere United Methodist Church while my husband, Bob, directed the church's choirs and attended seminary at Emory University's Candler School of Theology in Atlanta, Georgia. From the beginning, there was a special bond between the Eleys and the Bruces. Their children were almost our age, and we spent many evenings visiting with them and sharing good times. When our first son, Rob, was born, Allene and her children made a large banner that went across the front of the parsonage with the words "IT'S A BOY!" painted on it. As two students far away from home with a newborn, we felt affirmed and loved. The Eleys' youngest son, Bill, was in our youth group and sang in a traveling choral ensemble, The New Life Singers, with us.

Allene and her family touched our lives in many ways those three short years. I especially remember one early December when two of the tires went bad on our worn-out Chevy. "What will we do?" Bob asked me that morning. "We don't have any extra money right now. How will I get to *school tomorrow to take my exams?" That very day around lunchtime a check for $100 arrived in the mail with a note from Allene and her family: "This is what we are giving each child in our family for Christmas. You are like our children. Merry Christmas!"*

How could she have known that we needed $100 for tires?

Another evening that winter, Bob and I were homebound with the flu with raging fevers, coughing, and aching. Rob was just an infant. As we lay in bed trying to decide who would get up and feed the baby, the doorbell rang. There were Allene and her children with a steaming pot of chicken soup.

"Thought this might help you get well," she said matter-of-factly. "And by the way, we're taking Rob to our house for a few days until you get back on your feet. This young man needs to be rocked and fed."

And with that, her girls wrapped up the tiny baby and put him in their car, relieving us of added responsibility while we were so ill.

Bob graduated from seminary and we accepted our first appointment in Florida. Somehow we lost touch with Allene and her family. Through the years we exchanged a card or two; occasionally we received a newsy message through mutual friends. But that rainy Tuesday morning she was on my mind in a powerful way. Now, writing letters is not something I enjoy doing, but I had to respond to this nudge. I sat by the fireplace in our den and wrote her a two-page letter telling her about our busy family: "Rob is now a student at Emory University, Brittnye is a junior in high school, and Ashley (you never met Ashley!) is now in 7th grade ... Allene, how quickly time flies." I found an old address book and wrote Allene's address on the envelope, sealed it, and put it in the mailbox.

The next evening as I was getting ready for bed, the phone rang.

"Mrs. Eley? Sure, my mom is here." I heard my daughter say in another room. Mrs. Eley? Allene Eley? I quickly picked up the phone beside my bed.

"Allene? Is this really you?" I couldn't believe I was actually talking with this wonderful friend after all these years.

"Did you get my letter?" I didn't know how a letter could have been received so quickly, but surely that was why she was calling.

"A letter? Did you write me?" Allene was surprised that I had even thought of her. "No, I haven't received a letter. We came to Jacksonville early this morning. My dearest friend, Anne, died here on Tuesday. I couldn't wait to give you a call while I was in town and try to catch up on the years."

Allene went on to explain that her lifelong friend lived in the same city as we did. Anne had died on Tuesday—the very same day and time that Allene was on my mind, and the day that I wrote the letter.

We talked and talked that night, catching up on old times. She proudly told me of the accomplishments of her five children; many were teachers, and her son, Bill, was a physician and professor at Emory University—the same school our son now attended. She shared about the recent sadness she had faced: her husband of 50 years was now in a nursing home with Alzheimer's disease, and her sister had died just a few months before. "Debbie," she said. "This is the saddest time in my life. I've lost my three best friends this year— my husband, my sister, and now Anne."

Is that why God suddenly put Allene on my mind? Is that why I felt so compelled to reach out to her the day before?

"Oh, but Allene," I said with tears streaming down my face. "You have been blessed with so many more friends too." And with that I vowed to continue keeping in close touch with my friend from years past.

As I hung up the phone, I remembered the Scripture verse, "Little children, let us stop just saying we love people; let us really love them, and show it by our actions" (1 John 3:18 TLB). I thanked

*God that I had listened to His voice and followed
my thoughts with the letter.*

*Unable to sleep that night, I reflected on Allene's
sorrow. But I felt comfort in knowing how God's
mighty hand works in our lives. We are the precious hands and feet that respond when He calls
us to care for those who are hurting.*

Moving beyond Self

What is love unless it's given away? We've all heard
that statement before, but for women of vision, that statement is a challenge. Reaching out and caring for others
helps us to focus on something other than self.

Good intentions don't count. When you make time to
passionately care for those around you—reaching outside
of self to actually do something—you can make a difference
in the lives of family and friends and experience God's
"something more."

CHAPTER 8

Women with Vision Embrace Hope:

Connect to God's Plan

Deep within the hearts of most women today is an intense yearning for personal fulfillment and purpose in life. Don't spend another day looking back with regrets on the way you have lived your life. Learn from the past in order to live to the fullest in the future. Don't wait until it is too late to discover something more. Don't settle for being a frustrated caterpillar if you want to be a butterfly.

Writing a Eulogy

Use this time to write your eulogy. Grab a piece of paper and a pen, then take a minute to think about what you want people to remember about you after you die. What is the most important thing you can leave with them? Avoid the defeatist response that Satan wants you to adopt. He wants you to say that you will never be anybody great, so you will live just like you have been living and make the best of it. Woven throughout this book are the stories of every-day, ordinary women who gave themselves totally to God. They fought complacency. They survived transitions and crisis. They purposefully looked beyond their own situations and asked God to show them something more. You do not have to give up on a vision in the middle of adversity and suffer with an empty and unsettled spirit. There is hope in Jesus Christ. Don't wait until it is too late for you to be something more. Writing out what you want people to remember about you will help you know what is important to you about the way you live.

When our children were young, we told them they could be anything they wanted to be when they grew up. The same goes for you! It doesn't matter if you are 25 or 55 or 75, you can experience God's plan for your life to the fullest. Your future isn't "out there" somewhere. Your future is now.

We are not suggesting that you have to go out and move mountains or flash your name in neon lights. God's plan for you may be a quiet pursuit. As our kids would say, "Whatever!" Just do it! Take one step at a time.

Following is a vision-clearing checklist:

1. Find a quiet, safe place where you can think, reflect, cry, and be still.

2. Pray. No prescriptive phrases are needed. Just talk to the One who made you. He longs to listen. Ask God to open the doors so you can clearly see what He has in mind for you. If you are contented as a caterpillar, celebrate your role. If you desire more, seek it.

3. Read the Bible to learn all you can about God. He will give your life energy and direction.

4. Find another person you trust. Share your heart with him or her. Ask him or her to hold you accountable as you seek to follow God's direction.

5. Nurture yourself. Evaluate how you need to change and what you need to change in order to take care of yourself. Make a list and gradually check off each point as you move forward. The length of the list does not matter. If it takes you two months or two years, make a commitment to keep moving toward your goals.

6. When crisis comes, practice *Rest Stops for Resilience*. Breathe, relax, and look for God. Ask Him to turn your chaos into opportunity.

7. Let go of anger and fear. Unpack your baggage.

8. Compare yourself to no one. God created you to be you. Learn from others and ask God to help you adapt what you learn to make a difference in your life.

9. Think positively. Smile often. Laugh more.

10. Allow yourself to become passionate about life. Share your emotions and feelings with others.

11. Become a risk-taker. Walk that tightrope of life and experience the comfort of God as He helps you to stay balanced in the midst of fear.

12. Determine what is most important as you impact the lives of others. What difference do you want to make?

13. Grab on to hope and never let go.

14. Become comfortable with confidence.

How Clear Is Your Vision?

We spend much of our time in front of computers and books. It is critical that we are able to read and clearly see a computer screen. Ellen has struggled to find the right visionwear.

I have been nearsighted most of my life. But it was such a struggle when I noticed I was having trouble seeing things up close. For an editor and writer, the curse had begun! I tried several different kinds of visionwear and two eye doctors. Finally, I found an optometrist who was willing to work with me until we landed on what was best. Right now, I wear monovision, gas permeable, bifocal contacts. Monovision indicates that one contact is to correct farsighted vision and one is to correct nearsighted vision. Believe it or not, in my hurry, I often get them mixed up. It usually only takes me a little while before I realize what has occurred. My vision is not quite right. I can still drive and read, but my eyes hurt and everything is a little blurred.

As children of God, when our vision isn't right, we miss out on His blessings. We are forced to settle for second best. But the amazing thing about our God is His willingness to try again with us, even when He knows that we will still get things wrong and have to start over again.

Be Confidently Hopeful

Have you ever observed that every emotion can affect you positively or negatively?

Anger is a natural emotion that can motivate you to

bring about change if you channel it and don't allow it to control you. Happiness is a wonderful feeling if you avoid living in a dream world, believing everyone should make you happy every day. Working through your grief will help you understand pain and suffering in yourself and others. Grief that's not worked through can lead to depression and unresolved anger.

Some Christians believe that confidence and self-esteem are sinful. But they are gifts from your Creator who desires you to be a voice of strength for Him as He uses the gifts and abilities He has given you. Just as in every emotion, balance is called for to achieve the maximum benefit. We are not confident in ourselves alone. We are confident because we belong to God. We have a healthy self-esteem because God designed us to feel for ourselves in order that we might feel more for our brothers and sisters. We are confident in the future because God is in control. We are confident in the future because God made us and loves us just as we are. We are confident in the future because God calls us to hope. We have a future about which to be confident because our loving Father cared so much that He sent His only Son, Jesus, to die for us. His suffering, death, and resurrection have bought us a future with our Father in heaven.

We can respect others because we understand how to respect ourselves. We love others because we understand how to love ourselves. If you have ever been around someone who couldn't love or respect himself, then you know how vital it is that we first feel emotionally and spiritually healthy about ourselves before we can reach out to others.

Why do people choose to be fearful instead of confident and hopeful? Look at the reasons:

- People tend to think of hope as a romantic, whimsical emotion rather than a powerful, life-changing gift from God.

- People associate self-confidence with arrogance and pride. It is easier to feel fear than to remain confident and hopeful.

- Demonstrating confidence and hope invokes action. Fear immobilizes you. Society pushes the role of the victim and people buy into it. A victim gets more attention. Her hopes have been crushed in the past and she does not want to risk again. She refuses to trust God enough to hope.

Our Hope Is Built on Nothing Less than Jesus' Love

For God did not give us a spirit of timidity, but a spirit of power, of love and of self-discipline.
2 Timothy 1:7

As Christians, our hope and confidence come from God. Therefore, to be hopeful is to deal with God. To remain hopeful is to trust God. It is faith. Society would rather uplift the victims than the faithful. But there are major differences between victims and survivors. Victims need sympathy; survivors need congratulations. Victims are emotionally crippled; survivors move forward. Victims have trouble talking about what they have experienced; survivors have a story to tell. In telling their story, survivors begin to thrive. Invariably, their story helps someone else. It is a powerful cycle if you fight against the urge to become a victim.

Overcoming the Odds: Marjorie

Marjorie's son Chad was 10 years old when their life changed forever. Her son went riding with his dad one Saturday morning. As they returned home, a drunk driver hit them head on. The accident left Marjorie a widow with a quadriplegic son. The doctors told her that her son would not live much longer and should be put in a nursing facility. Marjorie did not know how she would manage, but she was determined to give her son the best care she could at home.

A decade later, Marjorie's son is graduating from high school. Either Marjorie or a special tutor has accompanied Chad to school every day for nine years. After several surgeries and months in the hospital, Marjorie and Chad moved forward. She refused to sit back and give up. In addition to learning the medical techniques necessary to care for Chad, Marjorie has overcome insurance battles, financial difficulties, school problems, and loneliness. She will admit that the years have been challenging, but she gives God the credit for sustaining them and giving them hope.

"I never gave up hope that we could make it," shared Marjorie. "The day Chad came home from the hospital, I committed to be there for him. We have been amazed at the people who have reached out to us even though we never asked them to. I just kept moving forward every day, every year, and now, here we are at graduation." Though usually shy, Marjorie has learned to share her story to inspire others whose lives are changed by disabilities. "I don't want it to seem like I am bragging, but Chad and I have worked hard together and I don't mind telling anyone about our achievements," voiced Marjorie. She and Chad have no idea what the future holds, but then they had no idea what the past would hold either. Chad graduated tenth in his senior class.

Marjorie could have given up at any point. She was a single mom with no college degree. She could have given up on Chad, on herself, on other people, and on God, but she chose to remain hopeful and press on. Marjorie's tenacity continues to influence children, adults, teachers, and law makers. In Chad's words, "I would not be here if it wasn't for my mom." Perhaps your crises will never be as difficult as Marjorie's. We pray that your faith in God will provide you with a hope and confidence to see you through any obstacle.

Find Your Hope Exercise

Go get your Bible; look up the following Scripture verses and mark them. Write the references down on a card and keep it in your Bible. When you need your hope and confidence renewed, read them again.

> *I love You, O LORD, my strength. The LORD is my rock, my fortress and my deliverer; my God is my rock, in whom I take refuge. He is my shield and the horn of my salvation, my strong-hold.* Psalm 18:1–2

For You have been my hope, O Sovereign LORD, my confidence since my youth. Psalm 71:5

Why are you downcast, O my soul? Why so disturbed within me? Put your hope in God, for I will yet praise Him, my Savior and my God. Psalm 42:5

Surely God is my help; the Lord is the One who sustains me. Psalm 54:4

Starting Your Hope Chest

Throughout this book we've discussed the negative effects of a poor attitude and pessimism. Negative feelings about yourself and about others zap your energy. Pessimism batters down your hope for the future like a relentless hurricane attacking a shoreline. Satan wants it to gradually consume you until you feel defenseless and abandon your will. He delights in your hurtful spirit. He smiles when you cut someone else down in order to feel better about yourself. He knows that other weak victims of pessimism are drawn like magnets to you. "The gossip groupies" will sustain you until they become jealous of you and will easily use you as their next target. Loyalty is not a virtue for a pessimist.

When our mothers and grandmothers married, they brought with them a hope chest, often made of cedar. It may have contained pillows, a quilt, and perhaps some family keepsakes. It held their hopes and dreams for the future. The chest protected its contents for years to come.

Protect your hope. Guard it well. A multitude of other people will batter your shores to tear you down with a negative spirit. Some may not even know what they are doing. They just want to protect you from harm. They don't want to see you get hurt. But you know that it takes risk to move forward. Hope is active. Hope gives you confidence. Hope keeps you alive. Hope allows you to dream and believe and succeed.

Ellen touches hope every day. Here's her story.

We all go through times in our lives when it is difficult to believe in ourselves and find hope for the future. God is so gracious to provide friends at those times to support us and care about us unconditionally. When I was experiencing a particularly difficult time, a wonderful friend sent me a very special gift. Good things do indeed come in small packages. I opened the package to find a small rectangular box. Inside of the mysterious box, I found three rocks. A word was etched on each rock. One rock reads, Hope. Another, Believe. And the other, Dream. I use them as paperweights so I touch them often through the day. God uses the rocks to steady me. When I renew my sense of hope in Him, then I begin to strengthen my belief in His purpose for me and I am free to dream again. And when I start to dream, I begin to hope my dreams will happen. When I dream, I take action to make my dreams a reality.

God made us with imaginations to create and dream. Any marketing company will tell you that the first step to producing a great, marketable product is the idea stage. Allow yourself to dream of possibilities. If your mind and heart are free to think in different directions, then God can lead you to new ministries and new people that you can add to your Hope chest.

Hope Breeds Courage

If you want to be strengthened by hope, read books about early twentieth-century missionaries whose courageous faith and work helped to bring the Gospel to the farthest reaches of the world. God used women like Amy Carmichael in India, and Bertha Smith and Marie Molsen in China to spark spiritual awakenings that resulted in thousands coming to know Christ. They boldly spoke out for Christ in the midst of wars, communism, famine, danger, and disease. They didn't do it to be written up in the *Ladies' Home Journal* Women of the Century issue; they did it out of a powerful, overwhelming commitment to God. They were gifted in evangelism and teaching, not because of some rare upbringing, but because of God's hand on their lives. They did not question their call based on denominational disputes. They dared to dream about the far-reaching power of the Holy Spirit. They were missionary visionaries used by God to change the world.

If you are thinking that you will never be a missionary in a foreign country where you face overwhelming challenges and the overwhelming outpouring of God's Spirit, stop. No one knows what the future holds. Your foreign country may be a move to a new city or a transition setback that causes you to start over. But God's outpouring of power and grace can be felt anywhere, anytime.

Who would ever have dreamed that the daughter of an unassuming watchmaker in Holland would contribute so much to God's worldwide movement? If you have never read *The Hiding Place,* read it. The triumphant story of Corrie ten Boom will give your hope new meaning and energy. You will cry and laugh and know that whatever the future holds, God holds the future. Corrie and her family were imprisoned in Nazi concentration camps during World War II because they hid Jews in their watch shop in Holland. What God miraculously taught Corrie and her sister, Betsie, will help you as you deal with handling loss, insecurity, illness, death, and difficult people. God used the courageous testimony of Corrie ten Boom to bring hope all over the world.

The Finish Line

When Corrie ten Boom and her aging, sick sister, Betsie, were imprisoned, they faced horrible difficulties. Invariably, it was Betsie who helped Corrie see the beauty of God's handiwork in the middle of the darkness. Betsie kept telling Corrie of a home they would go to when they were released from the prison camps. Her dream often brought them hope and temporary moments of peace. Ultimately, it was heaven that Betsie saw. It was the home that God had prepared for her. It was the mansion He has promised each of us.

Our time on earth is fleeting, temporal. Life is too

short to waste wishing for something more. Once your destination is secure, you have a steadfast hope. If you have put your trust and faith in Jesus Christ, you are heavenbound. It is your heavenly hope that motivates you to make the most of your earthly journey. As Paul said in 2 Timothy 4:7, "I have fought the good fight, I have finished the race, I have kept the faith."

Ask yourself these questions:

- What do I want out of life?
- What does God have in store for me now?
- Where is God at work and how does He want me to join Him in that work?

Our journey of faith has a two-fold purpose. One purpose is to go about our lives and honor God in everything we do, whether it's washing clothes for our families, running a company, or teaching in a school classroom. God wants to be there and use us in the routine days of our lives.

Our second purpose is to grow so close and so deep with God that we dare to ask if there is something more. When the routine ends, when the transition times come, when your heart desires to accomplish great things for your Lord, look to God for direction and for clear vision. We pray that through reading this book, your eyes have been opened to see more clearly than ever before. We pray that through the words, the Scripture, the testimonies of women from the Bible, from church history, and from today, you have found new strength and hope. We certainly did as we researched, prayed, and wrote. We could end this book with a touching story that leaves you on some emotional high, but that is not true to its purpose. Instead, you must write the ending. It requires introspection, prayer, and action. We challenge you to complete the following exercise as you reflect on what you have read.

- Write down the important things from the book that stand out in your mind.

- Of these things, which stirred your heart the most? Make a shorter list.

- Look at your short list and prioritize which things you actually want to start thinking about and praying about.

- Pull out your list of attributes from Chapter 2. Read over your strengths list and your prioritized list once each day for a week. Pray, sincerely asking God to clear your vision.

- Evaluate your daily routine. Decide what you want to stop doing, what you want to do differently, and what you want to start doing. Set goals and plot how to gradually reach each one.

- Read magazines, local newspapers, your church newspaper, and any other publications which promote the needs of others around the world. See what jumps out at you. See what stirs your heart even more.

Now take action with your clearer "eyesight"!

- Make a list of possible ministry actions that interest you and explore their possibilities.

- Talk to people involved in the ministry possibilities to get more information.

- Ask a trusted friend to pray specifically about your desire to follow God if He is leading you to something more.

- Get your feet wet. Depending on your time situation, either jump right into something, or map out how to gradually start or get involved in something. Remember, we are not suggesting you add busy work to your daily schedule. The message of this book is for you to discover your personal purpose and vision. God wants to bless you and use you.

Realize the Possibility and Promise

Abba, Father ... everything is possible for You. Take this cup from Me. Yet not what I will but what You will." Mark 14:36

As you finish reading this book, we want to leave you with this eternal message: Our Christian faith is a faith of hope. Realizing the possibility and promise of each day is one of the keys to successful Christian living.

Sometimes circumstances beyond your control will overwhelm you, and you may find it hard to have hope. When you feel like you are over the line and are experiencing burnout, ask God to reassure you of His presence.

Ellen remembers the months as a single mom in graduate school. She had to balance her time between class, a campus job, mothering, remaining active in church, staying involved in her children's school, and paying the bills. There was not much time for cultivating friendships or relaxing.

I would cry out to God and ask Him to show me some sign of hope that I could make it. I desperately wanted a visible sign that He loved me. God answered my prayer in an unusual way. I started parking in a different place and walking a further distance to class. The campus grounds were full of trees and squirrels. The scenery changed with the seasons. But it was a small bush that He used to give me hope. I passed the same bush every day all winter and then began to see tiny spots of green appear and grow each day. I made sure to check it every time I passed for more new growth. Each new leaf seemed to restore a small amount of hope within me. When it was in full bloom, I felt such strength and knew beyond any doubt that God loved me and was in control of my life.

Deb also experienced God's intervention repeatedly as she raised three children close in age.

My 3-year-old son, Rob, had been unusually cranky one day, complaining of an earache. While washing his hair, I pressed on Rob's ear, and it began to bleed. Thinking it might be swimmer's ear, I rushed him to the pediatrician. The doctor probed the ear, pulling out tiny, folded pieces of paper from the canal.

"Why did you do this, Rob?" he asked.

"I want to be a camera," Rob said. "I got paper and folded it like film. I put it in my ear, so my eyes could take pictures of what I see. My brain would develop them."

I was floored at what had occurred even as I watched this active child so carefully. But I must confess that even under the most watchful eyes, personal disasters occur and life seems out of control.

Raising three children close in age, life's interruptions are commonplace. In fact, I can recall times when I had barely come up for air when another calamity would occur. Like the time when the three put on their new overalls and went outside to our "safe" fenced-in backyard to play. Fifteen minutes later, I noticed them in the front yard and the gate was unlocked. Following a greasy trail of motor oil from the garage to the driveway, I saw 4-year-old Brittnye using a stick, trying to let the air out of the car tire. Her 6-year-old brother was pouring oil for 2-year-old Ashley to use as fingerpaint.

"We're playing mechanic," Brittnye said with pride as oil dripped from her tiny hands. "It was Rob's idea."

Both girls admired their older brother who was busy trying to mop up the oil on the driveway with the bottom of his new overalls. Life's interruption, or outright catastrophe? And that was just one day.

The longer I am a mom, the more I learn to take these calamities in stride—as part of life's uncharted journey. Whether it involved a charred dinner because I left the units on high; getting my 2-year-old up from her nap only to

*find that she peeled all the wallpaper off the wall
surrounding her bed; roaming the neighborhood
at midnight looking for the beloved pet rabbit; or
rushing to the emergency room with an asthmat-
ic child—personal disasters are unplanned and
disrupt your life.*

You must know that everyone—man, woman, or
child—faces stormy weather. Whether from unruly kids,
family difficulties, more month than money, or terminal
exhaustion, life's interruptions make you feel as if life is totally out of your control. There is only one remedy for these
interruptions: Jesus Christ. Real faith begins when we are
stripped of any humanly wisdom and pride. We fall to our
knees and pray, "Lord, You know my needs. I am a sinner. I
need Your forgiveness." And with that He smiles and says,
"Peace, be still." The winds cease, and there is calm.

Patiently Wait upon the Lord

Hope is tenacious and eternal, but we must have
patience as we wait upon the Lord for eternal signs to help
us hang in. We've been there. We've been women whose
vision was a bit blurred—physically, emotionally, mentally,
and spiritually. But we have also found new life with the
Great Physician. He sent a burning bush to Moses and a
budding bush to Ellen. He intervened again and again for
Deb as she felt overwhelmed with the task of motherhood.
As you patiently wait upon God, He will answer your
prayers and give you hope.

But this awesome power of God can only be seen if
you have an attitude of anticipation. As we talked about ear-

lier in this book, a Christian woman with vision keeps her eyes focused on Christ, her Redeemer. She has passion for God and feels His power. She prays, she persistently touches the lives of those around her, and she patiently waits upon the Lord. Perhaps most important, a Christian woman with vision is a possibility thinker!

You are a living promise of the goodness of our Lord. To "clear your vision," do not dwell in your past. Yesterday is gone. Tomorrow is not yet here. But today matters! Today is your day of discovery! Move forward with great anticipation and trust in the Lord!

Endnotes

1 Lewis and Betty Drummond. *Women of Awakenings.* (Grand Rapids, Michigan: Kregel Publications, 1997) Page 34.

2 Leo Buscaglia. *Bus 9 to Paradise.* (Thorofare: Flack Inc., 1986). Pages 136–137.

3 Ronald G. Nathan, Thomas E. Staats, and Paul J. Rosch. *The Doctor's Guide to Instant Stress Relief.* (New York, New York: G. P. Putnam's Sons, 1987) Page 39.

4 Brent Q. Hafen. *The Health Effects of Attitudes, Emotions, Relationships.* (Ashland, Ohio: EMS Associates, 1992) Page 255.